TEN
MYTHS
THAT
DAMAGE A
WOMAN'S
CONFIDENCE

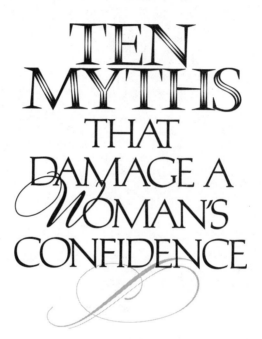

TEN MYTHS THAT DAMAGE A WOMAN'S CONFIDENCE

PATRICIA HOLT

BETHANY HOUSE PUBLISHERS
Minneapolis, Minnesota 55438

Published by Bethany House Publishers
A Ministry of Bethany Fellowship, Inc.
11300 Hampshire Avenue South
Minneapolis, Minnesota 55438

Printed in the United States of America.

Library of Congress Cataloging-in-Publication Data

Holt, Pat
    Ten myths that damage a woman's confidence / Patricia Holt.
      p. cm.

    1. Christian women—Religious life. 2. Self-esteem—Religious aspects—Christianity. 3. Self-esteem in women. 4. Self-confidence.
I. Title.BV4527.H66 1995
248.8'43—dc20   95–7497
ISBN 1–55661–379–2   CIP

*Dedicated to my wonderful
West Valley Christian Academy
staff and board of directors,
who spent their lives
radiating Jesus.*

PATRICIA HOLT is the School Administrator in a Christian academy. She has coauthored two books with Dr. Grace Ketterman: *Choices Are Not Child's Play* and *When You Feel Like Screaming*. Her *The Early Childhood Kit* won the 1983 ECPA Gold Medallion Award in Christian Education. She and her husband have two grown children and make their home in California.

Contents

God is worthy of trust. The better we know Him, the more we will trust Him. The more we trust Him, the more confidence we will have—a confidence founded in our unchanging, all-loving Father.

Myth One

Lord, I must confess, my expectations for myself, for other people—and, Lord, even for you—can lead to frustration and disappointment. I'm not where I expected to be at this time.

Mainly, I don't have the control of my life I expected to have. I don't feel as good about myself as I think I should. Where have I gone wrong? Is it me, is it others—or is it you, Lord, trying to tell me something? I'm very confused.

I believe you are the great and mighty God of the Bible— but you are not working in my life in the wonderful ways you worked in the lives of people in the Scriptures, because in their lives I can plainly see your plan unfolding. Can you give me a perspective on my life ... even a little?

"If I had better control of my life, I'd have better self-esteem."

ON JANUARY 17, AT 4:31 A.M., I lost any illusion that I have ultimate control of my life.

I awakened in the dark to a thunderous roar from far beneath the surface of the earth. It seemed as if the house was suddenly lifted from the solid soil and was being shaken up and down. Furious jerks and jolts nearly threw me from my bed. I could hear all our personal "treasures"—all that we had saved for, collected, and given to each other—crashing and tumbling as the roaring and rolling went on and on. I was certain that we were in the epicenter of the quake—maybe "the big one" that we in southern California have been expecting. I was terrified and feared for the lives of my family. My husband leaped out of bed. I screamed for my children—then cried, "God, help us! Jesus, save us!"

Beneath our feet . . . the wrenching of the earth had begun ten miles underground, and from there the deadly shock waves embarked on a long, destructive march. Inside hundreds of thousands of homes in the greater Los Angeles area, devastation accompanied each violent convulsion of the 6.8 Northridge earthquake that became one of the largest and most costly disasters in history.

And when the major quaking ceased, our family was left to grope for flashlights in the dark. There was no electricity. No water, gas, or telephones. We made our way to my parents' home. They were still alive.

Standing there together, still shaking, we rejoiced in the mercy of the Lord.

Then the aftershocks began.

The damage escalated with the thousands of jerks and jolts. More homes were destroyed. More lives up-ended. Our family, like many many others, slept in cars—just in case.

In this earthquake, dreams, businesses, homes, and lives were lost. The plans and investments of one or more generations were to reduced to rubble. Treasures became trash. Jobs were gone. The "California dream" was no more a reality.

Pastor Jack Hayford, of the Church on the Way in Van Nuys, expressed what was formulating in each person's mind: "I have no guarantee against future assaults on my peace."[1]

———— ∽ ————

The people of Los Angeles went into mourning. In the next weeks, friends said:

"I am mourning the loss of security."

"I don't have control of anything in my life."

"I don't know what to expect anymore."

"I never expected God to take my home or my business."

Do we realize how much our fragile reality is supported by the underpinnings of expectations?

In a message given two weeks after the quake, Pastor Craig Johnson of Westlake said: "Expectations are powerful, driving forces in our lives. They pervade every area of life. Although our expectations are not always rooted in reality, they continue to guide our lives. Every pain, every frustration, every offense, every hurt that you have sustained in the past month is a result of a failed expectation. You had a need. You expected someone—or God—to meet the need on your terms, and they failed."[2]

Not that all of our expectations are unreasonable, not by any stretch. I expected to be safe in bed in my home through the night. I expected to be in control of my schedule the following day. I expected to keep my possessions, until choosing to give them away. I expected—or at least hoped—God would allow life to go on without a natural catastrophe touching my family. And I must be honest, though it pains me to admit this one: In my heart of hearts I expected to be a protected "princess" who glided above the ugly realities of life.

Life is riddled with expectations, for Christians and non-Christians alike. We think: *If I can get control of my life, I will have self-esteem. The more control I have, the more self-esteem I will have. And the more self-esteem I have, the more in control of my life I will be.*

Somehow, we expect to gain control of our lives. Beyond all the techniques for personal management—from our Day-Timers to our goal-setting seminars to our financial-planning schemes—lies the shimmering image of a well-planned life of our own ordering. A dream life.

Don't the most successful and the happiest people plot and plan their own destinies?

We like to control our self-esteem—and it seems so reasonable. Everyone I know wants to have control of their life and feel good about themselves. So do I.

From the earthquake I learned firsthand that no human being can control God or any part of His universe at any time. And if our quest for self-esteem leads us—drives us—to the control of outside events, the quest is futile.

How strongly do you try to control your life? What happens when the way God decides to run His universe does not coincide with your expectations? What is your reaction?

All Too Human

Control is a big issue for all of us. I'll be the first to admit it's an issue for me. Attempting to control others is a trap many of us fall into, consciously or unconsciously.

Wives manipulate to get control of husbands—using food, sex, or trigger words—and men have their own ways of trying to control us. Mothers hug, cajole, and scream to control their children. Many women use the verbal and nonverbal trappings of friendship to control friends. Of course we don't call it control. None of us would ever do that! But check your response when you expect something from your husband, your children, or a friend and it's dashed. Do you experience stress, frustration, helplessness, anger, or despair?

So many of us have learned to work hard, with the expectation that the harder we work at anything of value, the more we will be rewarded. If we work hard at being a "good" wife, mother, friend, Christian, we will reap certain benefits: a responsive loving husband, obedient model kids, supportive friends—health, financial security, and inner peace from God. When one or more of these things is shaken we experience a personal "earthquake." Our sense of control is shaken—and so is our self-esteem. After all, if we had controlled things better, we wouldn't have inconsiderate husbands, kids who rebel, friends who betray— and a God who refuses to jump through our hoops. Right?

Hard to take I know, but some of us suffer the most serious blows to our self-esteem because we are so entrenched in our expectation that we can control our lives to a desired outcome.

What does it mean to be *in control*? It means that somewhere inside I think my world should go according to my expectations. Those expectations can be positive or negative. When my world is going according to my expectations for my husband, my children, my friends, my work, my home, my personal self, and I am getting the results I expect. My self-esteem gets a boost because I think I'm doing a great job. But when it's not, have you ever heard yourself ask, "What am I doing wrong?"

The great problem with our approach to self-esteem is

that it's result-oriented: It depends on the actions and re-actions of others, including God, to meet our expectations.

Let's explore this further. It seems to offer us the prize of inner peace once we've ordered and oiled our whole world as we want it to run. But at the same time control is exactly impossible.

The concept of self-esteem is deceptive. If self-esteem is the goal, low self-esteem is inevitable.

Yes, as adults we are challenged to manage our lives to some degree—and the lives of others. But there has been something of a "self-esteem" movement in our culture, and one of its two major errors is that it leads us to believe we can plan and control almost everything. The other pow-erful presumption that misleads many is this: Self-esteem is measured by how we feel—and that, like the ground, can shift at any moment. The major issue is how you or I feel about *ourselves* at any moment of the day or night.

I can tell you that I *felt* terror during the quake. After it was over, I felt initial joy that my family had been spared. Almost immediately, I felt sorrow for the loss of things I had treasured. I felt enormous frustration as I tried re-peatedly to put the house back together, only to have a se-vere aftershock throw things down once more. I felt alter-nating joy and sorrow as I heard that a friend was safe, but that their home or business had been destroyed. I felt anx-ious because the electricity, water, and gas were off for days. I felt anger because the food and gas lines were long. I felt depressed because stores that I had shopped in for years were closed. I felt a grief that a way of life, my way of life, a way of life I enjoyed and was accustomed to, was gone, never to return. I felt grief for those friends who have given up and left, searching for security in another place.

Each feeling was real and honest—but which one should I have planted my feet on? Which feeling was it that "made me feel good about myself"? Which feeling was it that raised my self-esteem? None of them. By the time I even identified a feeling, it was shaken by another circum-stance, to be replaced by another feeling.

On any given day, feelings can change so rapidly that it is difficult to keep up with them, even those feelings that come in the course of a mundane everyday life. I can wake up "feeling" okay. I can weigh myself and feel annoyed. Then I can look in the clothes closet or refrigerator and feel disappointed. What I want, what I bought, and what I thought it would do for me—well, it isn't there. One of "them" has eaten it. What I want to wear won't do for my appearance what I'd like it to. Phone calls can make me "feel" encouraged, frustrated, dismayed, stressed. And so it goes all through my day.

If you were to chart your feelings, I suspect you would discover peaks and dips, too. Do we honestly *want* to live this way? Feelings—as a stable base on which to live—just cannot be trusted. You and I have little control over what stimulates our feelings. We have less control over most of the events of life. Yes, our feelings are a true read of where we are *momentarily*. But the fact is, we are adults on a journey to a higher place.

The woman who attempts to build her life on the shifting soil of self-esteem will be frequently torn apart by the earthquakes of life. And earthquakes there will be. Isn't it time to move away from the unattainable goal of control as a way to "feel good about yourself"?

Yes, our feelings and expectations are human. But we don't have to be held hostage to feelings when they take us for a ride.

Getting Off the Roller Coaster

What can a woman do with her ever-changing feelings? Where can we go for security, for strength, for a reason to keep on when life shakes us to the core of our being?

What happened to our home in the southern Cal disaster illustrates a point—a good foundational point for all of us who want a new stability from within.

Many homes much farther from the epicenter than ours were demolished—but our home was not destroyed.

Yes, it was the mercy of the Lord, and there was another factor, too.

Structures built on a type of soil called "fill" were susceptible to huge shifts when the earthquake waves shot through with enormous force, and the soil kept on shifting long after the shock. Damage continued. But earthquake waves move faster through *bedrock* than through less stable filler soil, so the damage to structures built on it is less catastrophic.

Then I remembered. When we built our home, grading the hilltop we are perched on was extremely difficult. The jackhammers kept breaking. Finally the builder had to dynamite the ground so that our home could be built. Although our home sustained what is termed "cosmetic damage," the home suffered no structural damage—and that was because our home is built on bedrock. That was the only way it withstood the shaking of a 6.8 earthquake without collapsing.

Earthquakes come in life, for you and for me. They are inevitable. We cannot stop them, and we don't know when they are coming, or from which direction. By the time they begin, it's too late to prepare. We can only ride them out and endure. Sometimes they are tremblers. Other times the whole earth shifts, jolting our carefully built "structures" with destruction that is felt for a long time.

I Need a Rock to Stand On

Are you experiencing an earthquake now? What about the challenges that surely lie ahead? Perhaps you have already endured a severe shaking. Perhaps aftershocks are continuing to disrupt your life. You wonder if life will ever seem "normal" again. You wonder if you will survive—and sometimes even wonder if you *want* to.

How you survive depends on the "soil" that is undergirding the "house" of your soul. If your life is built on feelings and the need for control, you will shake and there will be breakage. But if you are built on the bedrock of a spiritual confidence in Someone greater than you, then you will be shaken, but you will *never* break!

As Christian women, we say that God is our Rock. We believe the words of the Psalmist:

> God is our refuge and strength, a very present help in trouble. Therefore we will not fear, though the earth be removed, and though the mountains be carried into the midst of the sea; though the waters thereof roar and be troubled, though the mountains shake with its swelling.[3]

We believe those words are absolute truth. We even sing, "On Christ the solid rock I stand, all other ground is sinking sand. . . ."[4]

We *say* the words. We *sing* the words. But we live our lives in contradiction of the words. Some would take a negative approach—but I believe it's because we are in a process called *growth*. We are growing as women. Growing in our spirits, too.

We are also growing in our knowledge of God. Our knowledge of God is too little. Our relationship with God is too shallow. You and I tend to focus on fragments of God here and there, and we let Him in to the bits of life we want Him in. (The rest of it we can handle very well on our own, thanks.) Is the shaking we feel in any way a wake-up nudge? A call to go deeper? I think so.

There is a big difference between a life that gives lip service to who God is, and a life that recognizes the power of God in each event of everyday life. Our growth in trust is a big part of the spiritual journey—moving beyond confidence in ourselves and our careful plans to a confidence that is settled in God.

I long to be a woman of "God confidence"—to live my daily life reflecting the truth that God is a Rock and a Fortress. I want to hold in my spirit the truth that every event of life's journey is an opportunity to become a woman who is growing in confidence because I am trusting more of myself to a God who is eternal bedrock.

Because the shifting soil of self-esteem is so deeply ingrained in most of us, I have written this book to contrast the things that destroy a woman's self-esteem with the bedrock of a life that is growing in godly confidence. Keep in mind it is a process: There is no quick and easy method.

Becoming a Woman of Confidence

Step by step, we can move out of confidence that is based in ourselves and the shifting sand of feelings, and into a life of greater freedom in spirit. You may find that God is already nudging you awake in one or more of the areas explored in the pages to come. That's great! Though changes and growth are a challenge for every one of us, we know it is out of love that God reaches into our very circumstances to wake us.

Do we always recognize that love of God that lets us know He is still with us in every shaking? Mostly I think we forget that little verse "God is love" when things are going at opposites for us. But sometimes, *often,* we can find the love of God trying to reach through to us in the midst of life's most trying problems.

And so, it is to the problem moments we must look first. Unless, of course, your life has no problems. . . .

Myth Two

God, I believe that you have forgiven my sins and that I'll be in heaven with you someday. But that's not helping me now. How can I feel so inadequate, when I know you? Why do my non-Christian friends appear to have more confidence than I do? It doesn't seem fair that their lives are more together than mine, when I have your Holy Spirit inside me. How can I lead others to you, when some days it's hard to face my own small world . . . or even face myself?

"As a Christian woman I shouldn't have problems."

A WOMAN'S LIFE IS NOT SIMPLE. It's made up of a complex web, a weaving of intricate relationships.

Each delicate thread represents something or someone we are attached to—a child, a friend, a parent, a place. Life stretches that gentle weaving, pulling the threads until sometimes it feels they will break. A child grows and changes . . . and leaves. A husband changes . . . for better or for worse. Time and circumstances move us on from the familiar and sweetly settled . . . to the unknown. Our lives begin to tear apart, and it seems no one understands the grief and apprehension, the anxiety.

Nearly every woman I know attempts to build her life in a way that will promote security and protect her from life's surprise assaults. Yet even the Christian woman who has woven a wonderful life for herself can have her world blasted by one of life's sudden earthquakes. Just as the Northridge quake struck without warning, there are many other shattering jolts that can unexpectedly change a woman's well-ordered life:

- A mother discovers her teenage daughter is pregnant.
- A husband leaves for another woman (or man).
- A young woman finds out that her best friend is experimenting with drugs.
- A single woman's fiancé abruptly "dumps her."
- A young mom is diagnosed with a chronic or terminal illness.

- A beautiful young girl's body is crippled by a freak accident.
- A wife learns her husband is slowly dying of a debilitating, incurable disease.
- A mom watches her home and worldly possessions burn to the ground.
- A single woman hears her biological clock ticking, but no man is in sight.
- A grieving widow discovers her late husband molested their children.
- A mother of four learns that her husband is losing his job.
- A mature woman must now assume full responsibility for her aging parents.
- A mom watches her child abandon family values for gang-related activities.
- A young woman's drug-addicted brother is threatening her home and children.
- A mother is given test results that indicate her child is dying.
- A girl's mom leaves home and family for another man (or woman).
- A wife and mother's ex-husband has been released from prison and is creating havoc.

These are some of the grim realities of life that women sometimes have to face.

Perhaps your struggles are less dramatic—but still difficult and debilitating. Each one of us has experienced the emotional numbness that settles when we feel totally inadequate for the challenges that assault our security.

Unseen Adversaries

After years of listening to women share their hearts, I realize that the vast majority of women do daily battle with a host of unseen adversaries. At any moment a woman may fall to the ground wounded, or deep insecurities may cause her to crouch low behind walls of personality, poise, or pretense. Although our insecurities take different forms, the bottom line is the same: "We do not have the confidence it takes to cope with the many and varied challenges we have to face."

The gaps in our confidence may differ. You may not be daunted by the thought of making financial investments, while I may be overwhelmed at trying to balance a checkbook. I may sponsor and arrange a community-wide gala, while you may hate the thought of having to entertain one couple for the evening. Beneath our surface differences lie some facts and inward reactions that make us all much the same. If you were to casually observe the following three women, they would not seem to have very much in common. As you will see, however, they are much more alike than they are different:

Veronica tries to blend in with her environment so she will not be noticed. She is so unsure of herself that she is afraid to speak up in a group or stand up for her own convictions for fear of being disliked, misinterpreted, or misunderstood more than she already feels on a regular basis. "What's the use?" she moans. "I've tried and failed for years. Can you believe? I don't even like to volunteer to make cookies, help decorate, or even be part of a committee. I know that if it comes to cookies, mine will be the worst-looking and the most blah-tasting. If it's decorating, mine will stick out and say, 'homemade by loving but incompetent hands.' So, why try again? I can't face the stress I feel when I don't measure up to other women."

Jennifer was well over thirty when she married a non-Christian. She is back at church, but her husband will have no part of it. He doesn't care if she and the children go, so she brings her two boys . . . who make a "lasting impression" on every single teacher and church worker.

Jennifer is paralyzed by embarrassment when she's around other Christian women who have a Christian husband and "good" children. She wants to hide and never go to church again. It's not worth the inner agony. "I don't even have the confidence to make my children mind," she berates herself. "How can I call myself a Christian when my life is a mess and I'm nothing but a failure?"

Ruth is hyperactive. Everyone knows it but her. Whatever needs doing, she does it, and she does it well. She can serve, lead, organize, and teach. Other women get tired just looking at her. Her home is in order, her husband is an elder in the church, and her children are well-behaved. And yet . . . she laments, "Sometimes I get so tired. Everyone expects me to *be*, to *know*, and to *do*—no matter what it is! But how can I say *no*? I'm expected to be the one everyone can count on to be dependable, faithful, and reliable. Something has to give. I can't stay on this treadmill much longer. My fuse is getting short. Lately I've blown it big-time when someone has challenged my plans or my authority. Then I feel ridiculous and terribly humiliated. I've got to get my emotions under control."

Are you a woman who is still a victim of circumstances? Do you continually compare your level of competency with that of others? Are you controlled by the real or imagined opinions of others? Perhaps you are a combination of all three of these women, or another type of Christian woman altogether. Regardless of our outward skills and the varying ways we manage some of our emotions, lack of confidence seems to be the great common denominator among women. Curiously enough, two powerful personalities from totally opposite ends of the spectrum agree.

In her book *Revolution From Within* the feminist writer, lecturer, and organizer, Gloria Steinem, made this confession:

> Just at the moment [of my greatest distress and insecurity] I got a letter from something called *The Keri Report: Confidence and the American Woman*—a nationwide survey of 6,000 men and women sponsored

by [the Keri] hand creme company. The letter informed me that I had been named one of the ten most confident women in the United States. It made me realize all over again what deep _____ women were really in.[1]

Over a decade earlier, Christian psychologist Dr. James Dobson conducted a study of over 5,000 married women between the ages of twenty-seven and forty. The majority were mothers who had small children and who professed to be Christians.

As he expected, "low self-esteem" was indicated to be "the most troubling problem" of the majority of women completing the questionnaire. Dr. Dobson says in his book *What Wives Wish Their Husbands Knew About Women:*

> This finding is perfectly consistent with my own observations and expectations: even in seemingly healthy and happily married young women, personal inferiority and self-doubt cut the deepest and leave the most wicked scars. This same old nemesis is usually revealed within the first five minutes of a counseling session: feelings of inadequacy, lack of confidence, and a certainty of worthlessness have become a way of life, or, too often, a way of despair for millions of American women.[2]

How would you rate on a "Confidence Check-Up"? Please take the next few moments to honestly answer the following statements. Your responses will help you identify your thought processes, understand how you see yourself, and focus on the areas that need to be changed or strengthened.

After each question, rate yourself in one of the four categories: Almost Always (A), Sometimes (S), Occasionally (O), Never (N).

1. I need reassurance, compliments, and   A S O N
   continual reinforcement from other
   people to feel confident.

2. I wonder, "What are they thinking about   A S O N
    me?"
3. As a Christian woman, I thought I'd be   A S O N
    more confident than I am.
4. Much of my life is controlled by the   A S O N
    opinions of other people.
5. I need a man in my life to make me feel   A S O N
    confident.
6. I say *yes* instead of *no* because I want to   A S O N
    be accepted.
7. I feel threatened by other women.   A S O N
8. I feel I can never be as good a Christian   A S O N
    woman as _____(fill in the name).
9. I feel vulnerable.   A S O N
10. I feel engulfed by insecurity.   A S O N

Totals for each column: _____

Multiply for grand total ×:   3 2 1 0

GRAND TOTAL: _____

Now, let's score your responses. Give yourself three points for every "Almost Always," two points for "Sometimes," one point for "Occasionally," and zero for "Never." Add up your total.

20–30 points—I have "lived" your struggles. Through my early years God allowed me to grope through an abyss of insecurity to discover a little of who He really is, and just what He can do with a life yielded to Him. I am excited about what God will do for you as we journey through this book together!

10–12 points—Perhaps you already have begun to implement the practical principles we will cover in this book. If so, then you will be encouraged to continue to develop God-confidence, and will gain further insights to help you understand yourself and your God.

0–10 points—Perhaps God has led you to this book for the purpose of understanding other women, learning how to increase your level of confidence, and sharing with those the Lord allows to come into your life.

Why is it important to "locate" our confidence gaps? I can speak to that from personal experience.

For many years I was the kind of woman who was insecure, anxious, vulnerable. I was a Christian who wanted to serve God, but I was leading a people-pressured life. I could not equate who I was with who I thought I was supposed to be based on the truths of God's Word. My life did not make any sense. And, for the most part, I was constantly wrapped up in myself and my problems. I lacked the confidence necessary to deal with daily life.

Frankly, reading the Bible only made me feel worse. All those great people! The adventures of heroes like Moses, Joshua, Joseph, David, Daniel, Hannah, Esther, Ruth. . . . Intellectually I knew that God is the same yesterday, today, and forever. But I didn't know how to connect the God of the Bible with my daily onslaught of problems.

As a result, I was tormented by my anxieties and inabilities for many years. I have since found that this tragedy is all too common. Professor and author Dr. David Seamands states:

> An uneasy sense of self-condemnation hangs over many Christians, like a Los Angeles smog. . . . Satan's greatest psychological weapon is a gut-level feeling of inferiority, inadequacy, and low self-worth. This feeling shackles many Christians, in spite of wonderful spiritual experiences, in spite of their faith and knowledge of God's Word. Although they understand their position as sons and daughters of God, they are tied up in knots, bound by a terrible feeling of inferiority, and chained to a deep sense of worthlessness.[3]

This was true for me, no question! The more I looked inside myself, the more I realized I simply couldn't be confident in myself. I couldn't rely on my own strength and abilities. Even when I was most secure and self-confident, something would inevitably happen to strip it away. Then I was left weak, helpless, and vulnerable again.

Although I had known Bible stories since I was a child, I became curious about the people themselves. How were these men and women able to do great things? How could they achieve? Were they just naturally loaded with self-confidence? Did they just look inside themselves and think, "I can do it, and I will"?

It was from the story of Moses that I began to find new direction and encouragement. In reading the familiar story of Exodus 3 and 4 again, it struck me that God spoke to Moses out of an ordinary desert bush, maybe a scraggly-looking thing with sharp edges where leaves should have been. Isn't it interesting that God used a dry, ugly bush to inhabit with His holy presence? *God can use anything,* I thought . . . *and maybe anybody.* I felt ordinary, unattractive, scraggly, with sharp edges. If God used an unsightly bush, could He use me? I kept reading.

The first thing Moses did was hide. Boy, was that familiar! I felt scared and ill-at-ease in new situations. Then the Lord spoke, telling Moses that he was the one chosen to deliver God's people. Moses continued to back away. He answered, "Who am I. . . ?" (I began to r-e-a-l-l-y like Moses.) He had no confidence at all. Perhaps all of his past failures and frustrations appeared before him, and he knew he never again wanted to put himself in a situation that would show off his weakness and inability to the world.

Then God assured Moses, "Certainly I will be with you. . . ." Even that guarantee wasn't enough. *Moses didn't want to do it.* The excuses began. I didn't blame Moses one bit. I understood. I hated being embarrassed. I despised being in front of even a small group of people. I couldn't speak in public.

Ultimately, Moses had to choose—between staying focused on himself, his weakness, and his *unwillingness* to come out of hiding in the desert—and the call of God. Apart from the particular task, what was God asking Moses to do? Simply to *trust*; and then to move out in a journey fraught with challenge, hard work, the need for massive amounts of planning, administration, good sense, judgment, people skills . . . *whew*!

The secret was this: Moses could only do this big task—or any small part of it—if he continued to trust daily in God's presence and direction.

Moses had to choose between confidence in himself or confidence in God. The Moses of the rest of the book of Exodus bears little resemblance to the Moses who wanted God to leave him alone. What made the difference? Moses swiftly learned to trust God for everything in his life. Moses discovered that God is worthy of all trust.

Being a person who lives and moves based on confidence in God is an "open secret" shared by all the heroes and heroines of the Bible. Some stories, like that of Moses, illustrate a complete lack of self-confidence and a phenomenal journey into godly confidence. Other stories, like Paul's, deal with a person who began with loads of self-confidence. Saul, as he was called before his conversion, was the kind of person I could never tolerate: He was brilliant and he knew it. He wielded his superior intellect and natural leadership qualities with arrogance. He used his privileged birth and outstanding educational opportunities and achievement to control. Of all the men in the Bible, Saul had to be one of the most self-confident and controlling. Humanly speaking, he was powerful, respected, and feared.

What did God do? He had to strip Saul of all self-confidence in order to replace it with godly confidence. Paul was thoroughly humbled by God before he could write in Philippians 3:3–7:

> Rejoice in Christ Jesus, and have no confidence in the flesh, though I also might have confidence in the flesh. If anyone else thinks he may have confidence in the flesh, I more so . . . but what things were gain to me, these I have counted loss for Christ.

Whether you have no confidence at all, some degree of self-confidence, or an overgrowth of it, there is a confidence that is infinitely better. It is a confidence that comes from knowing, trusting, and resting in God's abilities. Not in our own.

The greatest discovery of my life was the day I realized that I, Pat Holt, did not have to be confident in myself. I didn't have to rely on my talents and abilities, which seem so small when compared with others. In fact, I didn't need to be like anyone else. I could simply choose to focus on God, and He would give me His strength and His purpose, a little at a time, day by day.

No longer did my multitude of weaknesses matter. In one small and insignificant situation after another, God began to transform my life as I began to look to Him for absolutely everything. Whether it was finding my way in a difficult part of an unfamiliar city, learning a new skill, accepting a public speaking opportunity, or facing trouble in the life of one of my children—*I determined to trust Him.*

The following experience illustrates what God has done in just one area of my life—that of speaking in public.

As a little girl, I was painfully shy and self-conscious. I lived in dread of being called on by the teacher. I tried to hide behind the person in front of me so she wouldn't see me. On those terrible occasions when I was called upon, my mouth went dry, my brain went blank. I was humiliated.

I came to know Jesus Christ as my personal Lord and Savior in my early teens. And after being protected in a small Christian high school with a graduating class of about 50 students, I entered UCLA, which had well over 30,000 enrolled! Every one of those people seemed more intelligent, more poised, more articulate, and far more confident than I. It didn't seem right that all these non-Christians appeared to have it all together.

As a freshman, most of my classes were held in auditorium-style rooms, which held approximately 300 students. It was easy for me to slip in, escape to a seat in the highest section, farthest from the professor, and then quietly leave without being noticed. Unless someone spoke to me, I never spoke and never asked a question, not even of another student.

My freshman health class was a notable exception. There were about thirty students, and to my horror the teacher was determined to know each of his students and to have us know one another. Group discussion was mandatory. I was exceedingly uncomfortable and regretted being in the class. After the first session the chairs were placed in a circle. My discomfort intensified. Fortunately, there were an adequate number of outspoken students who seemed to love the sound of their own voices. For the most part, the teacher allowed them to monopolize each class session. This worked fairly well. Occasionally, the teacher would ask me if I had anything to say. I would mumble something foolish and then be left alone to listen and to wait for it to be over.

On one fateful day, though, the discussion turned toward God. I perked up. In prior sessions, there had been much talk of sex (in all of its manifestations), and this was a pleasant change.

One of the more aggressive students was complaining about a God "who could allow so much evil to dominate in the world." My heart began to pound. Another chimed in, degrading a God "who allowed innocent children to die." I thought, *I should say something*. But I was terrified. Immediately I knew, *I can't*. Another and another verbally skilled student added worldly wisdom in denigrating a God "who is supposed to be a God of love, but permits disease and death." Another student sneered, "How could a God of love send someone to a burning hell?"

Inside me a war was raging. If ever in my whole life I should speak, it was now. I was a Christian, saved by grace. How could I just sit there, and have the God of my salvation denounced over and over again? But I was so frightened. The urge to speak increased. But so did the overpowering fear.

The struggle inside me intensified. One voice said, *I must say something*. The other swiftly assured, *I can't*. A voice persisted, *I should defend my Lord and my God.* The other strongly insisted, *I can't.*

At about this time, I looked at the clock. It was nearly time for class to end. I knew that there would never be an opportunity like this again, yet I knew I could not speak. All I could do was to pray. *God, if you want me to do this, then you will have to give me your words and your strength. Because as you well know, I absolutely cannot do it!*

With sweaty palms and cotton mouth, I timidly began to speak.

I cannot recall my exact words. I do know that everyone was watching and listening, with surprise at my boldness. What they could not know is that I was the most surprised person in the room.

I told them about God's perfect creation and His intent for Adam and Eve in the garden. I told them of their choice to disobey and the consequences. I remember quoting John 3:16, "For God so loved the world that he gave his only begotten Son, that whoever believes in him should not perish but have everlasting life." In essence, while trembling like a cornered animal, I gave the plan of salvation!

Class ended. I assure you, there was no applause. Still shaking, and with weak knees, I rose to leave. The teacher asked to speak with me.

When we were alone he complimented me on my depth of my "religious convictions and belief system," but told me that in the future I would have to be careful of sharing so specifically about such a controversial issue! Then I walked out.

Nothing could hinder my joy. I did it!—No, not I, but Christ, in and through me! I spoke in public—to non-Christians—about the Lord. I never thought that would happen in my whole life. God gave me the courage! I was still stunned, but ecstatic!

Hours later, my breathing returned to normal but not my life. Never again would I experience the same level of terror in public speaking because I knew that if God wanted me to speak, then He would help me through it. I could count on Him. My trust began to grow.

Little by little, God gave me other opportunities to speak in public, but none of them stood out like that first one. Years later there was an interesting postscript that underscores what God can do on a life's journey of growth in Him.

I had been out of high school about fifteen years and was speaking to a group of several hundred teachers at a convention in northern California. After the session ended, a petite, perky older woman walked toward me with an uncertain smile. She hesitated, began to move away, but lingered until we were alone. I knew exactly who she was, a teacher in my former high school. She looked the same as she had then. She spoke first. "Excuse me, but did your name used to be Patty Arnebergh?"

I laughed and told her *yes*. We exchanged pleasantries. Then she explained, "I thought your voice sounded familiar, and you looked a little like the girl I knew but—you've changed so much. You never used to be able to speak in public. What happened to you?"

For an instant, I was taken aback. I had nearly forgotten my former fears. God had done so much in my life that now speaking in public seemed so easy, so natural. The Lord used this sweet lady to remind me of how much confidence I had gained through knowing and trusting the Lord in the years that had passed.

I want to clarify: Trusting in the Lord does not mean that things always work out in a way that makes you look good. But it does mean that focusing on the Lord and trusting Him gives everything a different perspective. You are not only seeking God's will but choosing to accept it on a moment-by-moment basis.

The purpose of this book is to lead you in the journey of becoming a woman who has confidence in God. Regardless of who we are, we need a bedrock confidence in God to deal effectively with the routine tremblers of life and to withstand the earthquakes. Since there is so much talk of self-confidence, I have coined a term that I hope you will not mind my using throughout this book. The term is "God-confidence."

God-confidence is the attitude of heart and mind that calmly, confidently believes God is sovereign and in control of all things everywhere at all times—and therefore He is worthy of trust without reservation. To be sure, this is a knowledge to *grow* in.

A God-confident woman knows that her sins are forgiven, that God is lovingly in control of her life throughout each day, that He is lovingly concerned for her well-being at all times. She knows He wants her to be strong, secure. Whether the outward task seems great or small in our eyes, she will be mightily used by God in her life.

God-confidence is the crowning possession of a Christian woman.

How does a woman acquire this godly confidence? Only by a process of learning to know God, to focus on Him in all areas of life—no matter what agonizing circumstances threaten. *God-confidence has nothing to do with the circumstances of life.* It has everything to do with learning to trust and wait on God when everything would tell us to give up in defeat.

Throughout this book I will share some of my continuing struggles in letting go of *self* in order to focus on *God.* We will also delve into the lives of many Christian women. Their stories are both heartwarming and heart-wrenching. Their honesty in dealing with their trials will challenge and encourage you in your journey toward becoming a woman of God-confidence.

One of the verses that will lead us along is Daniel 11:32. The words are so powerful and encouraging that I will quote it in three different versions. Choose your favorite, and memorize it. These true words will give you strength and increase your confidence in God in every circumstance.

> But the people who know their God will display strength and take action (NASB).

But the people that do know their God shall be strong, and do exploits (KJV).

But the people who know their God shall be strong and do great things (TLB).

An entire chapter is devoted to each of the major areas in a woman's life where lack of confidence in God can be a problem. These are: body image, health, accomplishments, finances, time management, men, and spiritual wounding.

But before we move on, please take time to consider the questions that follow in the section called "Reflections." You may want to write your answers in this book or elsewhere. Keeping this abbreviated journal will be a useful tool in helping you chart your emotional/spiritual journey toward God-confidence.

Reflections

1. Have you sustained a major "earthquake" in your life? Are the aftershocks still coming and continuing to prevent any return to so-called normalcy?

_____

_____

2. When did you first realize that you had a lack of confidence? Explain the specific situation(s) as clearly as you can recall.

_____

_____

_____

_____

3. Think about Veronica, Jennifer, and Ruth. Can you relate to anyone of them? Who?

_____

4. Of the ten statements on the Confidence Check-Up, which two stand out as areas in your life that need the most help?

_____

_____

5. Did your score on the Confidence Check-Up seem right to you, based on the way you see yourself?

_____

_____

6. Do you absolutely believe that the God of the Bible is "the same yesterday, today, and forever"? If so, how does that belief influence your thought patterns and affect your behavior on a daily basis?

_____

_____

If not, in what areas of your life do you not experience the strength that is promised to us in the Bible?

_____

_____

7. Looking back on your Christian life, can you see that Satan's deadliest weapon against you is a gut-level feeling of inferiority, inadequacy, and low self-worth? Explain.

_____

_____

_____

8. From what you have already read and experienced, how would you explain the difference between self-esteem and God-confidence?

_____

_____

_____

9. After you have memorized Daniel 11:32 in your favorite version, write it here.

_____

_____

_____

10. Begin to pray daily that God will make this verse and God-confidence a reality in your life in these three areas/situations/relationships:

    (a.) _____

    (b.) _____

    (c.) _____

11. Write your own "Heart Cry" to the Lord. Be open with yourself and the Lord. Remember, He knows and understands your hopes, dreams, and frustrations even better than you do.

_____

_____

_____

_____

_____

_____

_____

_____

Date of response_____

Myth Three

Father God! In my head I know that I am made in your spiritual image . . . but my heart nearly breaks sometimes when I look in the mirror and see so many physical flaws. Why is it so hard to face the fact that I'll never look like my ideal?

Sometimes I am around women whose looks I wish I had. I can feel a twinge of anger toward you—and I can feel envy settling in on me like a cold dense fog. I know it's ridiculous to struggle through a world that's filled with beautiful women—and if I don't come to terms in some way, I'll always be subject to having "perfect beauties" walk in and ruin my day. Will I never get over this tendency to compare?

"If It Weren't for Other Women, I'd Feel More Attractive!"

THE NORTHRIDGE EARTHQUAKE CAUSED great ground movement at the school where I am administrator—movement so severe that the cement foundation was cracked in nearly every ground-floor room. In some rooms, the cracking even caused the carpeting to split. In other rooms, the heaving of the earth caused part of the foundation to be raised, creating an uphill climb from one part of the room to another.

Needless to say, the school is not built on solid rock. Quite to the contrary. When the structural engineers measured the depth of the fissures in portions of the foundation, they discovered air pockets of up to *thirty feet* between the foundation and the earth in some places!

For the vast majority of women, our body image creates the foundation for how we feel about ourselves. Tragically, this foundational perception is generally not built on the solid rock of what God says in His Word, but on the deep and wide "air pockets" that the current culture builds. Even though beauty and attractiveness is subjective, the current standard becomes a woman's measuring stick.

Comparing our body image with that of others creates an earthquake that causes cracking, deep crevices, and wide chasms in our perceptions of ourselves. Then we are left to endure the internal damage.

The gifted illustrator Norman Rockwell was able to capture an entire story in a single illustration. The one that comes to mind is that of a girl of about twelve sitting on a stool in front of a full-length oval mirror. She is holding up a magazine that is opened to a full-page photograph of a very beautiful woman. The girl is earnestly looking into the mirror, comparing her face to that of the glamorous woman. It is obvious that she is wondering if she will grow up to look like her ideal. The look of uncertain longing on the girl's face indicates that she knows there will need to be a *l-o-t* of changes if that fantasy is to come true.

We can smile in recognition of these girlhood fantasies, but all the same seeds of dissatisfaction were sown and continue to be well-watered today as we browse through women's magazines, or watch those above-average lovelies in the movies. The roots of self-rejection grow deeper whenever we observe the deference with which "the beautiful ones" are treated. It's obvious that men's eyes—and too often their hearts—are drawn to them at our expense! Meanwhile, we are eaten alive with envy.

You can be assured that I was full of hopes and dreams for *my* body! How many of those dreams came true? *Zip.* Let me tell you about my perceptions of what God gave me versus the ideal I had created for the Pat Holt pedestal of beauty:

Blond hair—Yes, mine is natural, but hold the excitement! First of all, being a truly natural blonde has meant that I have absolutely no color in my eyebrows and eyelashes. As a frank-speaking relative once said, "Pat! You look sick without eyebrows and mascara!" Well, I agree, but I'd rather not hear about it. I *never* leave the house without the swift application of mascara and eyebrow pencil.

Another problem with natural blond hair has been that almost no one, other than a hairdresser, can comprehend a "natural blonde." Another relative used to attack my head from the back and roughly check for black roots while pulling out souvenir strands. Those "family times" remain as moments to remember.

What did I want? Raven tresses, of course—accompanied by dark, thick eyebrows and eyelashes!

Flat chest—Shopping for a bathing suit is a horrifying experience for almost the entire female population! But when you are tall and flat-chested, finding a bathing suit that hides your breast bones is a "Mission Impossible"! The good news? No matter what I wear on top, it is anatomically impossible for me to be immodest!

Of course hope in the human heart dies slowly. During the teen years I tried barbells, but only got a few bad toes from banging into them as they lay in wait in my closet. I never got an additional $\frac{1}{16}$ of an inch added to my measurement, or I might have endured the pain in my toes and kept going!

As I approached motherhood, hope for a rounded figure still fluttered in my flat chest. So many women told stories of what nursing had done for their breasts. Naturally I had to try. The gynecologist and pediatrician agreed after examining me, "It isn't the size of the bottle that counts." That was the good news, or starvation for my firstborn would have been inevitable. Well, I tried and tried and tried. By the time of the six-week checkup, my baby boy had not yet regained his birth weight. He was starving after all, so the doctors advised me to abandon breast-feeding, which I did. Immediately my son thrived. "What about my breasts?" you ask. Well, all I know is that I was flat-chested when I got pregnant, and after nursing all that remains are two nipples. Need I say more?

What did I want? That's easy. *Cleavage!*

Horrid skin—even as a little girl I never remember "liking my skin," but as an adolescent every emotion I had—bad and good—erupted on my face in the form of acne. I did not say pimples. I had a terrible case of acne, and it lasted for nearly seven painfully humiliating years! I was a challenge for dermatology, and faithful weekly visits to the dermatologist seemed to do little to stop the advancing ugliness. In addition to the shots and ointments and various experimental treatments the doctors tried, I avoided fats and oils. I got skinnier and more self-conscious, but the acne kept surging forward. I cried and begged my parents to let me stay home because of my ugliness. I was absolutely certain that no one in the world was uglier than I, and looking around at every other teenaged girl gave plenty of confirmation.

Well, dating and marrying a man who loved the Lord "with all his heart, soul, and mind" did wonders for my soul. Just as some of the inner *and* outer scars were healing, my son was born. Something must have happened during labor! As best I can guess, all the remaining oil in my skin must have seeped out during the delivery, and I was left with withering skin all over my body! From that moment on, I have been sloshing on various potions that are "guaranteed to make my skin younger" in a certain number of days. Right! It hasn't worked so far, and I'm here to tell you that I've tried every single brand on the market . . . just in case.

What did I want? The skin of *anybody* that has ever been photographed for a cosmetic ad.

I could go on about my body image problems *ad nauseam*. But as you've seen, the quest for "beauty" according to my body image ideal was a confidence *destroyer*.

Mirror, Mirror . . .

Does your body image "wish" match up with your body image "reality"? I'm certain you have your list of woes and grievances also. They may be different from mine, but they are discouraging, too.

For many women, unwanted pounds are the body-image nemesis. "Dieting is a national obsession in the United States. With nearly one-third of the population of the United States dieting, going on a diet, thinking about dieting, or recovering from dieting depression, journalists, medical doctors, physiologists, and the average-man-on-the-street all expound with equal fervor their pet theories on obesity. People are fat because:

they have malfunctioning glands.
they have a preponderance of "fat cells."

they don't exercise enough.
fat runs in their family.
everything they eat turns to fat.
they eat too much.
they eat too many sweets and carbohydrates.
they eat when they get nervous.

"The clue, of course, is that obesity results from calories ingested in relation to calories expended. Ergo: Lumberjacks eat mammoth amounts of food but stay relatively trim. A housewife, however, who eats like a lumberjack is a heart-attack candidate, and most likely miserably unhappy.

"And the more food she eats, the bigger she gets and the more she hates herself. The United States is a thin society. Ms. Average is constantly reminded on TV, in magazines, in store windows, and on the street that thin women are beautiful women. Fat women are ugly. Pills, belts, reducing machines, wafers, diet candy, diet soda, sugar substitutes, sauna baths, and calorie charts scream out the message that excess flesh is repugnant. The woman hates herself, is sure that other people hate her, and hides at home, ashamed of her body. But at the same time, she is convinced that she is pretty and that she would be gorgeous if only she weren't so fat."[1]

Judith Rodin, dean of the graduate school at Yale University and author of *Body Traps*, says, "Women are vulnerable to body dissatisfaction, and being pretty is no protection against it."[2]

"We live in an era when women are bombarded with idealized versions of what the feminine body is supposed to be," says Rita Freeman, author of *Bodylove*. "In many cases," notes Freeman, "a woman's weight can't be controlled any more than her height or eye color can."[3]

"Both Carol and Christine Alt were overweight when they went into modeling, but their body types were vastly different. When Carol was eighteen years old, she lost thirty pounds on a stringent diet of a single chef's salad a day. She shot to modeling stardom, gracing more than 500 magazine covers before turning to acting in the late '80s. She still looks trim, although she must stay on a careful eating plan to maintain that skinny frame.

"But for Christine the effort to get and stay thin was physically and emotionally devastating. Her insecurity about her large-boned body began in high school. 'I was always taller than everybody else,' she remembers, 'and I had big hips and a tiny waist. I felt awkward around all the girls in skin-tight jeans.'

"By the time Christine graduated, her sister had become hugely successful, and their firefighter dad urged her to become a model, too. When her big-name modeling agency told her to lose weight, Christine began what became a life-threatening battle with anorexia and bulimia. Once she survived on seltzer water for ten days straight, and she exercised obsessively, suffering memory lapses as her weight plummeted from 160 to 110 pounds. Carol remembers feeling frightened by her sister's behavior. 'Her figure was great, but her head was a mess. I saw the symptoms, but I didn't know what was wrong.' As Christine discovered, it's really tough to be cast as 'the heavy sister.' "[4] Judith Rodin adds, "It's hard to convince yourself that looks don't matter when we live in a society that rewards attractiveness."[5]

Let's say there is a history question based on a game show. Here's the question: The preamble of the Declaration of Independence written in 1776 says, "We hold these truths to be self-evident, that all men are created equal." That statement is meant to include women also. *Was there a woman represented in the group that wrote the Declaration?*

No woman would ever miss the answer: Absolutely not! Because every woman alive knows that it is *not* true. We are definitely not created equal.

Studies on beauty raise a number of rather ugly findings. In a sad little test of the importance of good looks, Pennsylvania scientists painted a large purple "birthmark" on the face of a woman and sent her out to ride an urban subway. At a stop for Philadelphia's Temple University's emergency medical center, she was instructed to throw herself down on the subway car floor in an apparent epileptic seizure.

"We wanted to see how long it would take before a Good Samaritan helped her," said Albert Kligman, a professor of dermatology at the University of Pennsylvania. "Instead, the car just emptied out right over her. We tried it three different times and no one ever helped her."

Of course when her face was mark-free help came readily.

"It pays to be good-looking in this country," Kligman said during a session of the American Association of the Advancement of Science. "Appearance is so important to our opinions of other people it's almost disgusting."

And baffling to scientists. In a recent gathering to explore the "Science of Beauty," they expressed their astonishment at how important attractiveness is in human relationships.

"When I started doing research, my goal was to show that attractiveness was not important," said Judith Langlois, a psychologist at the University of Texas in Austin. "But I've been unable to show that. Attractive individuals, adult or child, are always preferred."

Langlois has found that American standards for beauty remain remarkably consistent, almost unchanged by differences in race, education, or sex.

"Eighty to 90 percent of people agree on what is beautiful," she said. "In social science, that's an absolutely astounding number."[6]

I realize that all this can be subtitled, "Our Worst Body Image Fears Confirmed!" And we're not quite finished! Accomplishment seems to be no substitute for being beautiful. At the end of her life, Eleanor Roosevelt was asked if she had any regrets about her life. Her poignant response: "Just one. I wish I'd been prettier."[7]

The voice of the world shouts at us: "You are not measuring up!"

Oh sure, as Christian women we can say it is ridiculous to allow ourselves to become so pressured and controlled by vanity. Yet Satan successfully assaults even Christian women with feelings of inferiority, inadequacy, and low self-worth as we continually check out other women.

When *Glamour* surveyed readers about beauty, more than 6,000 women painted a complex and contradictory picture. Please answer the questions in this mini-version of the original survey, and let's see how your opinions compare with theirs:

1. Do you feel there is too much pressure on women to improve their appearance? Yes/No

2. Are there times when you make no effort to look good? Yes/No

3. When? At home/At work/On a casual outing/With the family only/With a good girlfriend/On a vacation/While feeling blue/Other (name them)

_____

_____

4. When do you make the most effort to look good? (Check all that apply.) At work/When I'm with my mate or partner/For a party or important work function/When I need to cheer myself up/Other (name them)

_____

_____

5. I am likely to make a bigger effort to look my best: For an important occasion with a man/For an important career occasion/Other (e.g., weddings, black-tie events, office parties, etc.)

_____

_____

6. What do you feel is the most important attribute for

being beautiful? (Prioritize from 1 to 4, 1 being the most important and 4 being least important). Beautiful face/ Great body/Gorgeous hair/Flawless skin.

---

7. Do you feel beauty is a form of power? Yes/No

8. I enjoy the time, effort, and money I put into my appearance. Yes/No

Here is how the responses looked on the *Glamour* survey:

1. Is there too much pressure on women to improve their appearance? 83% said *yes*!
2 & 3. When do you make no effort to look good? 83% said when they're at home/ 58% said when they're feeling blue/ 34% said when they're with family only.
4. When do you make the most effort to look good? 47% make the most effort to look good when they need to cheer themselves up.
5. I am likely to make a bigger effort to look my best . . . 60% of women over 35 make the most effort to look good not for their partners but at work; whereas 69% of women under 20 make the most effort to look good for a mate.
6. What is the most important attribute for being beautiful? 52% say a beautiful face/ 27% say a great body/ 16% say flawless skin/ 5% say gorgeous hair.
7. Do you feel beauty is a form of power? 85% said *yes*!
8. I enjoy the time, effort and money I put into my appearance. 84% of women say, *yes*![8]

Although there are contradictions galore in these responses—and maybe in yours, as well, perhaps the contradiction that most influences our lives is this: Although we feel pressured to conform to the beauty standards of our society, and deeply resent that pressure, we keep on struggling and striving. Why? Because of the deeply ingrained belief that beauty is a form of power. That power implies that we will receive the approval of people who will, in turn, affirm us, and "make us feel good about ourselves."

Curiously enough, it is the *mind* that determines how we "see" ourselves, not the mirror! Leo Tolstoy said it well: "I am convinced that nothing has so marked an influence on the direction of a man's mind as his appearance, and not his appearance itself so much as his conviction that it is attractive or unattractive."[9]

Recent studies only corroborate what Tolstoy knew so many years ago: 95% of adult women overestimate their body size, and 45% of underweight women consider themselves to be overweight.[10] Yet we must realize that the image we hold of ourselves in our mind is our reality—regardless of the truth, it is what we see in the mirror. I think we can say with assurance that beauty is more in the mind of *the one beheld* than in "the eye of the beholder!"

"Our physical self is a living part of us," Gloria Steinem says. And I agree. "Illness, aging, injury, or anything that shakes some pillar of our identity can unsettle it for a time. Even such subtle things as someone telling us we 'look rested' or 'look tired' can shift our body image for that moment.

"But the big difference is that if we have a basically positive feeling about our bodies and ourselves, we don't 'catastrophize'; that is, we don't extrapolate from a negative event or comment, from the effects of illness or aging, to a devastating feeling of despair about the whole self. With a basically poor image, on the other hand, each blow becomes proof that our bodies (hence ourselves) are defective or worthless, each compliment is interpreted as a friend's kindness or insincerity, and each day becomes a challenge to conceal our real selves (that is, what we think we look like) behind a facade. If they saw us as we 'really' are, we believe, others would reject us."[11]

How are we to get positive and stay positive, given all the challenges to our body image? The goal is to be so God-confident about our appearance that we can get our mind and attention off ourselves, to focus on God and to do the work God has given each of us to do.

Nine Steps to God-Confidence in the Area of Body Image

First, be honest with God. He knows your thoughts and feelings. Nothing is hidden from Him, and He loves you unconditionally—regardless of how angry or dissatisfied you may get.

Growing up, Sunday school teachers would often warn, "Remember, God sees your heart, so watch out!" At first I bought into that, thinking, "Oh no! How terrible! God sees my heart. God knows everything I've ever thought! I can't hide anything." But after I came to know the Lord, I found that thought so comforting. "God knows everything I'm thinking and He *still* loves me." I realize that God can cut through all the foolishness. He knows me, understands me. I never need to pretend with God. There is absolutely nothing that will separate me from the love of God—as Romans 8 tells me in clear terms. So you and I can always be dead honest with God in a way that would probably turn off the other people in our lives. That realization, in itself, is very important in becoming a woman of God-confidence.

And another thing. God understands all about the love affair people have with looks. In 1 Samuel 16:7, talks about the Lord looking on the heart, God gives a tremendous insight into the cult of human beauty. Samuel had just met one of the sons of Jesse, named Eliab. One look at this hunk and Samuel said, "Surely this is the man the Lord has chosen!" (TLB).

I love the response of the Lord: "Look not on his countenance, or on the height of his stature; because I have refused him: for the Lord seeth not as man seeth; for man looketh on the outward appearance, but the Lord looketh on the heart" (KJV). *Thank you, Lord.* What comfort and encouragement!

Second, ask Him to give you the wisdom to be your best. He cares. After all, Matthew 10:30 says that even the hairs on your head are numbered.

I have shared a few of my body-image frustrations in this chapter. Over time, as I got to know the Lord better by spending time in His Word and talking with Him in prayer, I came to the conclusion that if He really loves me as He says He does, and if He made me the way I am for His purposes, then He can help me to be my very best in all areas.

So I began to talk to Him about specific areas of concern.

I brought up the issue of my hair. Well, God led me to a great hairdresser, one that knows and loves the Lord. I asked the Lord to give her the wisdom to help me to get a becoming style that was manageable. Over time Lisa has patiently worked with me, teaching me how to help myself. My hair has never looked better.

When we are honest—and ask Him for help—we see what He can do. Choose to focus on Him and trust Him for the answer—even in the area of appearance.

Third, ask Him to give you appropriate goals for each area of appearance that concerns you.

How about a really small example? I love nails that are manicured and well-groomed. What do I have? Peeling stubs. No matter what I ate or didn't eat, what hot oil massage I used, nothing ever worked. I would wear some type of polish to get through the day and they still caught on everything.

No, my nails did not suddenly become beautiful and strong. But the good news is, I found a manicurist who is cheap (which means, I can afford to go), who understands my problem and knows how to camouflage what I have to give me smooth, strong nails. Now I don't have to take the time to struggle futilely with them.

I believe the God who created heaven and earth and all

that it contains answered my petition. Did I pray just one little quickie prayer and wait for the magical answer? Absolutely not! But every time I began to think about my nails and fret and fume, I would talk to the Lord about them, believing He was really the only one who could help me.

Fourth, trust Him to do good things for you and with you.

We have talked about rather superficial areas of appearance. Many people suffer disfigurement brought on by birth defects or tragic accidents. Joni Eareckson Tada is a triumphant example of what God can do with a fully yielded life.

Joni was an athletic teenager, with a beautiful face and body, who became a quadriplegic as a result of a freak diving accident. Joni knows from personal experience what it is like to want to die and not even be able to help yourself to do it. Thank God for not allowing her to be taken. She is known and loved around the world as an artist, author, and singer—an inspiration to everyone who struggles with disabilities.

It has been my privilege to meet and know Joni. As she speaks, her beautiful face glows with inner radiance and gives deep and fresh meaning to what she says: "I still don't know all the answers. My accident was not a monkey wrench that the devil threw into God's plans for my life. Far from being knocked off guard, God was not even frustrated by the devil's schemes to shipwreck my faith through my accident. God seeks our good and His glory. God steers that ship in such a way that all things work together for good."[12]

What God has done in and through the body, mind, and soul of Joni Eareckson Tada is magnificent. She has chosen to trust the Lord, and He has blessed millions of people as a result. Why I can walk and run but Joni can't, I don't know, but "I know whom I have believed, and am convinced that he is able to guard what I have entrusted to Him for that day" (2 Timothy 1:12, NIV).

Fifth, ask Him to make you content with who you are and how you are.

Contentment is particularly difficult for women in the sensitive area of body image. At the end of his life, the "father of psychiatry," Sigmund Freud, asked, "What is it that women want?" He didn't know. But I do, as do all other women. The answer is simple in terms of body image. "Just a little bit more (or less) than we've got!"

Neva Coyle is founder of Overeaters Victorious, author of *Free to be Thin,* and President of Neva Coyle Ministries. She endured a raging battle with wanting to be thin, and nearly did not live to tell her poignant story. I will recount some of it here:

> I started dieting seriously at the age of twenty-five. Though I was overweight, I was healthy, married to a man who loved and accepted me the way I was, and I had three healthy children, all of average weight. There was no other reason to diet except that I wanted to be thin: appearance was the only reason. I was in for some big discoveries. I learned that the dieting world has a language, a set of rules and a culture that the non-dieter never experiences and, therefore, cannot understand.
>
> I read all the diet books I could get my hands on and bought every magazine that had a diet article featured on the cover. Research sent me scurrying to buy recommended gadgets and even more books. I bought even Bible study books having to do with weight loss. While attending a study group based on one of these books, I was stabbed with pain when the leader said she'd once been as big as a size 14. I was, in fact, paying quite a bit to be a size 14.
>
> By this time, my whole mentality toward food had changed. Diet foods became a way of life for me, eating into an already-strained grocery budget.
>
> A little success was wonderful. But the moment I relaxed my efforts a little, up went the scale. I began exercising. Into the house came an exercycle, a rebounder, and a treadmill. I also joined an exercise

gym. When exercising failed to give me forever-weight-loss, I consulted several doctors, one of them a bariatrician. He understood my desire and need for weight loss and gave me pills. "They're covered in my fee," he explained, "you won't even need to stop by the drugstore on your way home."

Taking the rainbow-colored pills, I became high. I never ate, never stopped talking. I lost the promised pound a day—but I also lost sleep and friends and drove my family crazy. When I finally stopped taking them I slept for almost two weeks, and I got hungry.

Then I joined a support group. I'd been missing the empathy of other people—that was it. Hope returned. I felt I'd found help at last. I was no longer alone. I dieted faithfully, began losing weight, and discovered that it was okay to lose a little—but lose too much and others felt threatened.

Then I discovered weight loss by another method: surgery. I decided to have an intestinal bypass. I would no longer have to diet. I could eat like a normal person and, more importantly, feel like an accepted, attractive person after all.

In effect, I did not lose very much weight. Unexpectedly, I found myself sick every six months with blood clots, kidney stones, and other conditions that could be life-threatening. In a year, I had to have my gall bladder removed.

At that desperate point in my life, I started Overeaters Victorious. I had cut down to 850 calories per day and lost forty-five pounds in four months. I was thin! I was happy! But I was already sick and didn't even realize it.

Ten years later, with an established ministry to overweight people, and with my book *Free to be Thin* climbing to the one-million mark in sales, my health had deteriorated. Emotionally, spiritually, and physically I was a wreck, experiencing a high level of pain most of the time. Tests, X-rays, examinations, and endless interviews brought the shocking news: I was dying of malnutrition.

I lived in a daze of denial. Could I really die if I didn't have corrective surgery to reconnect the intestinal bypass? That was the prognosis.

I prayed. Friends prayed for me. I cried to the Lord. I also got a second medical opinion. Unfortunately, the verdict was even worse this time. "The truth is you are already in a downward spiral," the doctor warned. "Life will be increasingly painful. You can reverse the process—but you can't delay any longer. You can choose life, or keep going downhill, Neva. No one can make the decision for you."

Even now, there was only one big question: *Would I gain back all the weight?*

The doctor stared at me. "This is not a decision to be thin or fat, Neva. This is a decision to live or die. Either way, there will be consequences. But—yes, in all the cases I've read about, reversing intestinal bypass will cause the patient to regain weight. Possibly, you will regain all that you've lost, maybe within the first six months."

It is impossible to describe the guilt and pain. I felt like nothing but a big disappointment to all those in OV for whom I was supposed to be the model of godly discipline. Somehow, though circumstances were beyond my control, I'd let them down. Would they forgive me?

In the end, of course, there was little choice. While waiting for the surgery my spirits plummeted. I wondered if God was finished with me. After the bypass surgery was reversed I had to face a long, difficult recovery. It began with nineteen days of hospitalization and misery, as my system learned to digest food all over again. My only real salvation was God's comfort. One particular day, as I sensed I was fighting for my life, I experienced His presence in a way that I cannot describe. When it was over I knew God was fully with me—that He knew what was happening to me and He would never leave me or reject me. I had chosen life, even if it meant living and serving Him while overweight, and He would honor and bless that choice.

As my health returned, so did my weight. But to this day, I live with a sense of purpose and future because of having gone through those difficult experiences.[13]

Without the indwelling power of the Holy Spirit, contentment is virtually unattainable. But, "Is anything too hard for the Lord?" (Genesis 18:14, NIV). Isaiah 55:8 says His thoughts are not our thoughts and His ways are not our ways. I believe that if you and I present our bodies as a living sacrifice to the Lord, He will transform us by the renewing of our minds so we can "prove what is that good, and acceptable, and perfect, will of God" (Romans 12:1–2, KJV).

Contentment doesn't mix with anxiety. When you and I are anxious and worrying and fretting, we are not content! No wonder the Lord tells us in Philippians 4:6 to "be anxious for nothing." God knows we can't be content, which is His will, and anxious at the same time. So what can we do? Our gracious Lord gave the simple answer in the rest of the verse. "In everything by prayer and supplication, with thanksgiving, let your requests be made known to God." Isn't that great! God wants us to unload on Him, the burden bearer. That makes a lot of sense. After all, we are the "sheep of His pasture," and sheep are not burden-bearing animals.

If and when we do that, Philippians 4:7 promises that "the peace of God, which surpasses all understanding, will guard your hearts and minds through Christ Jesus."

Too often my attitude is, "Why pray when I can worry?" To be content, we must discipline our minds to give every single burden to the Great Burden-Bearer and trust Him with the result.

Sixth, ask Him to encourage you regarding your appearance.

That is a perfectly legitimate request. God not only cares about every little thing concerning you, but He is also thinking about you every moment of the day. (See Psalm 139:17–18.)

As you have already seen, I take the entire Word of God very seriously and very literally. I really believe it is God's love letter to me, and I read it that way.

One thing I do in this area is to really talk to the Lord about my dreadful skin. The shriveling and the withering and wrinkling is not exactly one of the big "uppers" of my life! But it's what I've got. It's what I must live with, and therefore I need encouragement—a lot of it—from the Lord in taking care of the yards of skin I've got.

I pray about which lotions and creams to use. Some I've tried are pretty good. No, they don't give me the "cover girl" look I'd like, but they keep me from depression, and that's good.

God, in His infinite graciousness, has helped me to find makeup that is affordable, and has guided me to lovely women who have patiently showed me how to apply the stuff. The greatest part is being able to put it on, and then forget about myself and focus on others!

Seventh, ask Him to deliver you from self-consciousness and self-absorption, and to deliver you from comparisons. Second Corinthians 10:12 warns, "But they, measuring themselves by themselves, and comparing themselves among themselves, are not wise."

Comparing ourselves with other women is the fastest slide to discontent, depression, and disaster I know. It is such a deadly and effective weapon, hitting the victim every time. No wonder our archenemy, Satan, uses it so often. The antidote? Keeping our focus on the Lord. When I talk to the Lord, think about Him, and read His Word, I am encouraged. When I look at others and compare myself with them, down I go.

Eighth, praise Him for what He *has* done, *is* doing, and *will* continue to do in your life.

Psalm 22:3 assures us that the Lord inhabits the praises of His people. The Lord commands us to praise Him. Why? Because He is worthy of all praise, worship, and adoration, and because He knows that we need to praise Him in order to enjoy optimum physical, emotional, and spiritual health. Doubt it? Try it! The next time you are "bummed out" about your appearance (or anything else), think about some verses of praise that you have memorized. If you haven't memorized any, then read a Psalm or two. And once you've tried it, a lovely lifelong habit may begin.

Ninth, remember that it's OK to get discouraged. In each area of your life, Satan will attempt to demean and repudiate your growing God-confidence.

The building of God-confidence is like changing any area of life. As Charles Swindoll so brilliantly articulated, it will be "three steps forward, and two steps backward." So what? Progress is being made.

God will not give up on you. Continue to ask Him for help, wisdom, strength, hope, and courage.

Reflections

1. What were some of your girlhood fantasies of body image?

_____

_____

_____

2. Name your major frustrations about your appearance.

_____

_____

_____

3. Have your frustrations been self-esteem destroyers because of your comparisons with other women, your self-concept, or because of the looks/comments of others?

_____

_____

_____

_____

4. Have you felt pressured to conform to the beauty standards of our society? Why? or why not?

_____

_____

_____

_____

5. Do you know of any beautiful Christian women who perceive themselves as unattractive? Perhaps you are one of these. Why do you think this is so?

_____

_____

_____

6. Carefully review each of the nine Steps to God-confidence in the area of body image, and write a personal comment on each one. This will be of great encouragement to you.

Step #1 _____

_____

Step #2 _____

_____

Step #3 _____

_____

Step #4 _____

_____

Step #5 _____

Step #6 _____

Step #7 _____

Step #8 _____

Step #9 _____

Date of response_____

Myth Four

Dear heavenly Father, I feel so low so much of the time. This has gone on for so long. It seems the world is just passing me by. The worst part is being exhausted all of the time. I wake up, and I'm too tired to even think clearly, much less do all the things I need to do, and all that's expected of me. Somehow I limp and drag through the day, so very weary and worn. When was the last time I felt excited, enthusiastic, and full of energy?

What I am feeling now is worthless! Is it always going to be like this? Then count me out. Why live in a world when I am nothing more than a limp, withered nothing?— You see, Lord, self-pity has moved into my being. I know that shouldn't be, but it is. All I can think about is myself and how badly I feel.

You are the Great Physician. Please restore me to full health and strength. Wouldn't I be far more valuable to you if I had lots of energy? I just can't understand why you don't want me healthy and strong. Please do something to help me.

"When I Don't Feel Good I Can't Help but Get Depressed."

CHRONIC HEALTH PROBLEMS CAN BE like that for a long, long period in the life of a woman. The obvious effects of a virus are usually "cosmetic." The sore throat, runny eyes, congestion, sneezing, coughing, and hacking last for a short while, respond to treatment, and then disappear, at least for a time.

The most serious and debilitating ailments are often hidden, difficult to diagnose, more difficult to treat. And they can leave her feeling empty, useless, condemned.

There is no way to discuss the difficulties of being a woman without mentioning the Big Four. Puberty, Pregnancy, PMS, and Menopause. The way I figure, one of these is either coming or going—and whichever it is, being bloated, moody, uncomfortable, and generally bent-out-of-shape is part of the "Wonderful World of Womanhood"!

No wonder my family hears these words shoot out of my mouth on a regular basis: "You know, it's not easy being a woman!" It's become a family joke. (I'm glad *they're* laughing!) The truth remains: Being a woman, in a woman's body, is difficult. Add on a chronic health challenge, and it is very, very hard to accomplish all that's asked of us and all that we *want* to do, without nearing physical and emotional collapse.

Some of the serious health problems that are guaranteed to destroy a sense of self-worth are:

- multiple major surgeries over a short period of time
- one or more physical disabilities

69

- chronic, debilitating disease
- constant pain
- permanent fatigue
- declines and limitations of aging
- being the caregiver of an ill, impaired, or deteriorating person.

Yet all these common and critical afflictions can become the reality around which our lives turn. What then? How do you cope?

It's easy to be "up" and "positive" when we feel good, and when our loved ones are healthy and bright. "Self" can do it. Who needs God-confidence? It's when we're bone weary, weak, and totally helpless that we can begin to learn about just who God really is. It is only when "self" comes to the end of all those personal strengths we "esteem" that we can begin to experience the magnificent emotional and spiritual healing of God-confidence.

Here is a little poem that states it so clearly:

> If all were easy, if all were bright,
> Where would the cross be, where the fight?
> But in the hard places God gives to you
> Chances for proving what He can do.

Perhaps God-confidence can nowhere be so strongly developed than when our physical strength is challenged. Let's look at some heroines who are becoming jewels of God, in my book, as they build the beauty of God-confidence from the physical ashes of poor health.

Jayni

Jayni Romero is an extraordinarily beautiful young woman of twenty-three. She has long, auburn hair, lovely features, and a slender figure—she appears normal in every way. But from the time Jayni prematurely entered this world, weighing in at a paltry two pounds, good health has eluded her.

As a little girl, Jayni was plagued with chronic strep throat, among numerous other maladies. She recalls an early memory. "I looked out the window watching my brother play. I wanted to play too. I asked my mother over and over, 'Why *can't* I play?'" Tears and tantrums did not make it better. Jayni was seldom well enough to play like other children.

At sixteen she was diagnosed as having Active Fibromyalgia. This explained the inflammation of muscles that caused constant pain, migraine headaches, tremendous weakness, and an ever-present sleep disorder. Jayni's reaction? "I'm young. I'm going to fight this!" And she did—for two years—with no result except an intensification of symptoms and a further diagnosis of Systemic Lupus Erythematosus. The vomiting every morning brought her weight down to under 100 pounds, she could not sleep, and became, in her words, "horrifically suicidal. I was consumed with forcing myself to just stay alive."

By the age of twenty, Jayni now relates, "My rage at God was overwhelming. I wanted to know *why* He wouldn't heal me if He was really God. I wanted to know *why* He was letting this happen to me. My increasing physical limitations intensified my rage. Still nothing happened. In time my rage transferred to indifference. I withdrew totally from God. I could not tolerate any mention of God. I found no comfort in any word from the Bible, or from anyone claiming to know God."

Jayni has used the vehicle of poetry to capture some of her feelings. Her poem entitled "Somewhere in Between" expresses her emotional state.

> Walking around in a vacant parking lot
> With a hollowed out head
> And hollowed out eyes,
> Sometimes I wonder if I'm alive.
> Or am I dead?
> Or somewhere in between.
> Maybe "purgatory" or in a coma,
> Attached to a machine with a tube down my throat—

Forcing me to breathe.
I don't want to breathe,
I just want to lie in shallow breath
With nothing but eternity touching me.
It seems easier to lie like a stone
Than to try to act alive
Or figure out
If I'm somewhere in between.

"And yet," Jayni says, "even in the midst of this, I knew that God was not giving up on me."

Now, three years later, the diagnosis has expanded to include a listing of eighteen different and specific illnesses. Each of these has myriad complicated effects. Jayni must take an array of strong medications, each having a host of potent side effects. Pain, weakness, fatigue, and sleep deprivation are ever-present. Her health has deteriorated, and although her growing limitations have adversely affected any "self-esteem," Jayni's God-confidence is growing. "My rage at God has turned into a rage to live! I am becoming increasingly tender toward the Lord. Even though I feel as if I live in the middle of hell so much of the time, James 1:2–3 is becoming real to me: "Consider it all joy, my brethren, when you encounter various trials, knowing that the testing of your faith produces endurance" (NASB).

"How much I've learned! God has used my pain and affliction to give me what few people can understand who have not experienced it. Through my pain, I have learned love, patience, and compassion. There is almost nothing that people can go through that I have not experienced. Maybe not the exact problem, but the feelings. I can understand more of the love and suffering of Jesus on the cross."

How does someone like Jayni face the future? "I have a trust factor with God I have not had before. That's the bottom line. The God I thought was out to harm me, I now trust. My severe limitations forced me to that. I take each morning as a new day. I may wake up with no hearing. I may end up in a hospital bed with organ failure. I do not know. But I do know that God is leading me by the hand. I will trust Him."

What about Jayni's mother, the mother who loved her and prayed for her before she was born? The mother who has spent a great deal of her life with her daughter in doctor's offices, in emergency rooms, in hospital rooms, and who will continue to do so. The mother who has pored through medical journals and *Physicians' Desk Reference* with her daughter in an effort to know and to understand. The same mother who recently lost her husband of more than thirty years. I asked Norma, an attractive redhead, the mature original of her daughter, Jayni, what keeps her going. She answered without a moment's hesitation, speaking slowly, distinctly, and with great God-confidence: "Philippians 4:13. 'I can do all things through Christ who strengthens me.' He has seen me through everything so far, and I know He'll see me through whatever comes next."

Sharon

Sharon Welles is another heroine. I first met Sharon more than twenty years ago. She was on staff in the children's ministries of a church that was exploding in numbers. I can recall Sharon as an energetic, enthusiastic, petite girl with soft brown hair, bustling around the church with love and laughter. Her gifts of teaching and organization were extraordinary. Within a few short years, God blessed her with a wonderful husband and two tiny tots, who were being reared in "the nurture and admonition of the Lord." Truly an ideal family!

Then her orthopedic problems began. The pain and swelling in her joints made mobility intolerable. The specialists agreed. Surgery was indicated. Neither the doctors nor Jim and Sharon could have imagined how many major orthopedic surgeries there would be. In a period of thirteen months, Sharon endured seven major orthopedic surgeries! There were eleven within six years, and others that followed. Pain was her constant companion—neck, shoulders, elbows, knees, back.

In talking with Sharon, she shed fresh tears as she recalled the immense physical and emotional trauma of those years. "The hardest part," she explained as she wept, "was not being able to experience the joys of motherhood. During the thirteen months that I had the seven surgeries, my children were five and eight. I couldn't cook, clean, go on bike rides or walks like other mothers. I remember when they got an opportunity to go to the Hollywood Bowl. Naturally I was invited, but couldn't go because I couldn't walk. Yes, that was my lowest time. Without the Lord, I probably would have committed suicide."

I could not help but wonder how she survived emotionally and spiritually. "The key is *attitude*. How you respond makes all the difference. I had to trust God and to accept that He knew what He was doing. Oh yes! It was hard. Constantly—and not only daily, but hourly—I had to give it all to Him or I could not have survived. Isaiah 26:3 was my verse, the verse that kept me trusting and focusing on the Lord: 'You will keep him in perfect peace, whose mind is stayed on You, because he trusts in You.'

"Focusing on that verse gave me amazing peace. I would realize just who God is, and appreciate what Jesus did on the cross. I had to learn to say *thank you* at the lowest times. Of course it was so difficult, so confusing. I would wonder, *God, why me? How can you use this? Why are you saying* no *on ministry,* no *on family?* On and on my mind would go. Each time, I had to reel it in. Jeremiah 29:11 would come to me: 'For I know the plans that I have for you,' declares the Lord, 'plans for welfare and not for calamity to give you a future and a hope' (NASB).

"Always, always, I had to go back to *trust*. I would forget, slip back, then go back to trust again. I would just cast all my care on Him because He cares for me (1 Peter 5:7).

"Gradually, I began to accept that *I don't have to know why!* I began to learn that not only am I totally dependent upon the Lord, but that I can trust Him all the time for everything. I also began to learn that the more I let go and let God, the more He can use me."

At this point, Sharon gave that familiar laugh I so love to hear and said, "You know, it's good for me to have remembered all this. *Trust*. That's what was important then and that's what's important now!"

Phyllis

Loving someone who has a debilitating disease, and caring for that person is another form of pain and suffering.

Phyllis Lowe is a tall, dynamic, very bright lady. She walks almost as fast as she talks. Before the question is asked, her answer has been completely formulated. She is positive and to the point. Want a straight answer? Ask Phyllis. She is also well known for her loyalty. You can be sure if she has something to say about you, she'll say it first to you, then defend you behind your back.

I wondered what kind of an interview I'd have with her. She rarely mentions her home situation and never seeks sympathy.

When Phyllis married nearly thirty years ago, there was not a shadow on the horizon. At six feet, four inches, strong and virile, Les made a great husband for Phyllis. Both were educated and accomplished. Such a bright future lay ahead. Two lovely children came. The only weakness Les ever seemed to exhibit was a stiffness in his hands and poor circulation. This would show up with the children.

"When he touched their faces," Phyllis recalls, "it would hurt them, because he would claw. Of course he didn't mean to, and wasn't even aware. How could I tell him not to touch the children or why? It was hard, very hard."

When the children were preschoolers, more serious problems began. While bowling, he would sometimes drop the ball. He'd become exhausted mowing a "dinky" lawn.

Then the diagnosis came. Les had a rare form of MD (Myotonic Dystrophy) that is peculiar to adults. Although MD itself is not fatal, eventually all the voluntary muscles are affected. When they are too wasted to perform their functions in respiration and circulation, death results. Fear and disappointment gripped Phyllis. "I cried my eyes out. I knew I'd never be able to do the things with my husband that my parents did in later years, things like travel. The next year and a half was a low point for me. It was my lowest spiritual point. I told the Lord, 'God! This is not fair. Why are you doing this to me, to my family?' This kept up for a long time. I withdrew in coldness from the Lord. Gradually I realized this attitude of mine was not helping. I could not change the situation. I returned to the Lord for help, peace, and comfort, and He was there for me."

As the disabling disease has progressed, Phyllis says, "I never think of the next step. I can't look ahead. I live day to day." At this point, her husband cannot open a door or carry anything. He spills everything. "It's tough in the bathroom," Phyllis says with candor. The routine tasks of bathroom functions have become a difficult family chore. "I don't mind putting on plastic gloves to do whatever I have to do. But I have to admire his desire to try to keep doing things for himself, even when it would be so much easier if I just did it, rather than to have to clean up all the mishaps. I respect his struggle for dignity. That's why the whole family allows him to try to do whatever he attempts.

"Mentally he's becoming extremely negative and talks nonstop. Even when the TV is on, he talks incessantly. It's tough. Right now, the hardest struggle for me is being a good wife. I believe that marriage means absolute commitment, and every day my commitment is on the line. I don't cry often, but when I do, I go to my room and cry alone and for a long time. I know that Jesus is the solid Rock, and I cry out for strength and for patience!

"You should have seen the stares when our family walked into a restaurant on Mother's Day. My dad has advanced Alzheimer's, my aunt has Multiple Sclerosis, my husband with MD, two young adult children, and me. What a group!"

What encouragement would Phyllis give to women facing similar situations in their homes? She responds enthusiastically, "How do I put up with it? 'Because He lives I can face tomorrow!' "

The Challenges Ahead

In addition to these serious health issues, there is the absolute certainty that—if we live long enough—we'll find ourselves in old age. In her book *Necessary Losses*, Judith Viorst compellingly describes the losses of old age:

> Although aging is not an illness, there is a slow-down of physical functions and an increase in physical vulnerabilities which may bring a zesty, full-of-life sixty-five-year-old to his knees by the time he hits eighty. There are physical impairments that can render us, against our will, dependent. There are organic and irreversible diseases of the brain over which neither courage nor character can prevail. And even if we aren't assailed by arthritis, Alzheimer's, cataracts, heart disease, cancer, stroke, and all the rest, the body has multifarious ways of reminding the octogenarian, "You are old."

Malcolm Cowley writes in his book *The View From 80* that such messages are delivered

- when it becomes an achievement to do thoughtfully, step by step, what he once did instinctively.
- when his bones ache.
- when there are more and more little bottles in the medicine cabinet.
- when he fumbles and drops his toothbrush (butterfingers).
- when he hesitates on the landing before walking down a flight of stairs.

- when he spends more time looking for things misplaced than he spends using them after he (or more often his wife) has found them.
- when he falls asleep in the afternoon.
- when it becomes harder to bear in mind two things at once.
- when he forgets names.
- when he decides not to drive at night anymore
- when everything takes longer to do—bathing, shaving, getting dressed or undressed.
- when time passes quickly, as if it were gathering speed while coasting downhill.

A gerontologist adds this: "Put cotton in your ears and pebbles in your shoes. Pull on rubber gloves. Smear Vaseline over your glasses, and there you have it: instant aging."[1]

My parents are octogenarians. When I mention self-esteem in regard to aging, they smile. "Looking in a mirror when I'm away from home," my mother relates, "I have wondered who that old frail woman with a cane is . . . and then I remember—it's me." My father recalls seeing his bent image in a window and being amazed at how he has changed. "Just ten years ago, I could run around the tennis court and keep up with people half my age. I know that time is over for me. The most discouraging part is knowing you won't get better."

Yes, aging has a way of stripping away the vanity and pride of earlier years. How do the elderly cope with their inevitable physical losses in addition to watching their friends die one by one? "Jesus becomes nearer and dearer. Only God does not change. Everything and everyone else changes, leaves, or disappoints. The Word of God becomes more real with each passing day," my parents proclaim with confidence. "And we are becoming homesick for heaven. We want to be with Jesus, to see His face—and to get those glorious new pain-free, wrinkle-free, limit-free bodies!"

Confident in Physical Limitation

This is how we might summarize the steps to God-confidence in the area of health concerns:

First, be free enough to ask *why*. Be patient enough for God to answer. God doesn't get weary of our moans, groans, and complaints like people do. I find it most interesting and comforting that with each person who is triumphing in the area of health problems, the first step toward a victorious attitude is honesty *and* patience with God. I believe this is just as important with the routine concerns of bronchitis, bladder infections, or PMS as it is with life-threatening diseases.

Second, learn what it means that God is sovereign. He rules in every circumstance of life, including every cold, cough, ache, and pain. He is in control. He allows infirmity for His purposes. He has allowed each of us to be in the condition we are for the reasons that are sometimes apparent only to Him. At those times it helps to know He is the great I AM.

Charles Spurgeon, a successful preacher of the 1800s, was considered to be the "Prince of the English Pulpit." By the time he was twenty-one, his sermons were appearing in annual volumes, which continued being published for sixty-three years—including twenty-six years after his death. To this day Spurgeon remains history's most widely read preacher and most prolific Christian author. Yet, until his death at age fifty-seven, "he was plagued with depression, discouragement, illness, and fatigue. Added to his own difficulties, he had the sorrow of seeing his wife become a semi-invalid at thirty-six. He admitted to frequently finding his strength unequal to his zeal. But he never let go of the promise that God's grace was sufficient for him."[2]

His remarks regarding health are most revealing. "I think that health is the greatest blessing that God ever sends us, except sickness, which is far better. I would give anything to be perfectly healthy, but if I had to go over my time again, I could not get on without those sickbeds and those bitter pains and those weary, sleepless nights. Oh, the blessedness that comes to us through suffering!"[3]

Third, God is able to heal. Remember that Scripture tells us in many places, such as Psalm 103, that God is able to "heal all your diseases." It is absolutely correct to ask for healing, for freedom from pain, weakness, and from the physical, mental, emotional, and spiritual debilitation that poor health brings. In Psalm 6:2–3, David pleads for healing: "Be merciful to me, Lord, for I am faint; O Lord, heal me, for my bones are in agony. My soul is in anguish. How long, O Lord, how long?" (NIV).

I have often found that I never truly appreciate health until it is taken away, even for a short period of time. I am totally unaware of the importance of a muscle until I pull it. Then every move anywhere in my body seems to relate back to that muscle that I didn't even know I had. "Pain is God's megaphone," C. S. Lewis said. Patsy Clairmont, Christian humorist par excellence adds, "If that's true, then, folks, I've heard from heaven!"[4] We can echo a hearty *yes*!

One thing is absolutely certain. Dealing with even minor afflictions gives us a sensitivity toward others. Spurgeon tells this story: "I once knew a minister who had never suffered pain or illness in his life. I was unwell in his house, and he most kindly tried to sympathize with me. He did it almost as wonderfully as an elephant picks up a pin. It was a marvel that he could attempt a thing so altogether out of his line. Many of the trials which are experienced by Christians are sent as an education in the art of sympathy."[5]

Fourth, when God does not choose to heal He will offer us comfort and—if we wait and pray—the understanding of His higher ways. The Lord said *no!* to Paul, even after Paul pleaded fervently and repeatedly for relief. Instead, God answered, "My grace is sufficient for you, for my power is made perfect in weakness." Then Paul was able to say, "Therefore I will boast all the more gladly about my weaknesses, so that Christ's power may rest on me. That is why, for Christ's sake, I delight in weaknesses, in insults, in hardships, in persecutions, in difficulties. For when I am weak, then I am strong" (2 Corinthians 12:9–10, NIV).

God didn't heal Paul, but he did heal Job. And we know that Job's affliction had nothing to do with his sin. Spurgeon states strongly, "It is an atrocious lie that some have uttered when they have said that sickness is a consequence of the sufferer's sin. I could not select, out of heaven, choicer spirits than some whom I've known who have not for twenty years left their bed, and they have lived nearer to God than any of us, and have brought to him more glory than any of us. Although we deeply sympathize with them, we might almost covet their suffering, because God is so greatly glorified in them. All over the world there is a brave band of these burden-bearers."[6]

Humanly, we cannot understand why God heals one but not another. We cannot comprehend why some are never ill, and why others have continual poor health. We cannot comprehend why some have ghastly accidents that cause total life changes for the entire family, while others seem to float through life on a protected cloud with silver and gold lining. We cannot comprehend the ramifications of birth defects and the like.

During this kind of shaking, it is crucial to know the God who "is the same yesterday, today, and forever" (Hebrews 13:8). You and I must accept the truth of Isaiah 55:8–9: " 'For my thoughts are not your thoughts, nor are your ways My ways,' says the Lord. 'For as the heavens are higher than the earth, so are my ways higher than your ways, and My thoughts than your thoughts.' "

Fifth, we must choose to *trust* the Lord. He loved each of us enough to send His only Son to live, suffer, and die on the cross for our sins. He is preparing a place for us that "eye hath not seen, nor ear heard, nor entered into the heart of man the things that God hath prepared for them that love Him." This same Lord is doing what is best for each of us, with eternity in view.

Isn't it interesting that in each story in this chapter *trust* became the bottom line and the path to peace and joy?

Tim Hansel has lived with continual physical pain for over a decade as the result of a climbing accident in the Sierras. His outstanding book *You Gotta Keep Dancin'* begins with this chilling revelation: "I can't remember when I last woke up feeling good. Each morning continues another layer of nauseating pain, stiffness, the dull gray ache, and the never-ending fatigue. It's been a little over ten years since my accident. Life was different before then; I just can't remember what it felt like."[7]

Tim has trod the rugged road to trust. "I have a plaque, sent to me during the most difficult period of my entire life, that says the following:

> Tim,
> Trust me.
> I have everything
> under control!
> Jesus

"It was sent by a friend who knew that I needed that reminder. Ironically, the glass got broken during shipping. I have never replaced the glass because, to me, the message is even stronger behind shattered glass."[8]

And that is true for you and for me also.

Sixth, out of our weakness—physical, mental, emotional, and spiritual—can rise His marvelous strength. Our "God chose the weak things of the world to shame the strong" (1 Corinthians 1:27, NIV). I am so thankful that you and I can and will be used by Him to do all things He has planned for us. Our weakness is no hindrance to Him, but often enables His strength to flow stronger and purer.

Fanny Crosby knew the sting of life's unfairness. Her blindness was the result of an incompetent doctor's prescription of hot poultices for an eye infection she contracted at six weeks of age. In one of her best poems, "Samson and the Philistines," Fanny captured the agony of blindness:

> O, to be left at midday in the dark!
> To wander on and on in moonless night!
> To know the windows of the soul are closed,
> And closed till opened in eternity!
> They who have felt can tell how deep the gloom,
> And only they who in their soul have learned
> To walk by faith and lean on God for help,
> To such a lot can e'er be reconciled.[9]

As Fanny learned to accept her blindness, and to trust the Lord, she came to believe God would turn the blindness into blessing.

The sorrows were multiple. In their book *The Hidden Price of Greatness*—which showcases such heroines as Fanny Crosby—Ray Beeson and Ranelda Mack Hunsicker write, "Fanny certainly understood about having sorrow on top of sorrow. In addition to her blindness, she grew up fatherless and in poverty. Her heart nearly broke when she had to say goodbye to her mother at fourteen in order to get an education. As a young woman she was grieved as her mother's second marriage was torn apart by a cult. The stress on Fanny became so great at one point that she became ill and had to leave her teaching position.

"She also suffered in her marriage to a man she rapidly grew away from in interests and friendships. Her marriage eventually ended in permanent separation. This sorrow, as well as the death of her only child, hurt too much for Fanny to share with anyone but God. The opportunities for bitterness were plentiful.

"But Fanny was not bitter. What was the secret of her remarkable endurance? 'One of my earliest resolves . . . was to leave all care to yesterday, and to believe that the morning would bring forth . . . joy,' Fanny explained. The lines of her songs were her lifelines in this pursuit. Out of her broken heart came the words from 'Blessed Assurance':

Perfect submission, all is at rest,
I in my Savior am happy and blest;
Watching and waiting, looking above,
Filled with His goodness, lost in His love.

"Fanny was not repressing memories and emotions; she was burying them in the ocean of God's love. 'The Lord planted a star in my life,' she said, 'and no cloud has ever obscured its light.' He had answered her prayers in a way that exceeded her highest aspirations. No wonder her motto was 'Trust God and Take Heart.' "[10]

Seventh, ask God for wisdom in how best to use limited energy resources. So often, the "good" is the enemy of the "best." When you and I ask the Lord to guide our energy choices, and to guard us against making poor choices in using our time and energy, He will. With God in charge, it is truly amazing how much He can accomplish through us—even with all our limitations!

Joni Eareckson Tada, whom I spoke of earlier, is *truly* one of the most inspiring persons I have ever met. As if being a quadriplegic were not enough for one person, Joni's health took a turn for the worse two years ago. She had blood pressure problems, drastic weight loss, infections, and stubborn pressure sores that forced her to lie on her back for two months at one stretch. If anyone ever had to ask the Lord to guide and guard her energy choices, it is Joni. And she does. And He gives her direction. Joni has written seventeen books, broadcasts a brief radio program five times a week on 695 religious broadcasting outlets, has done considerable guest speaking, is the head of her organization, Joni and Friends, has made four record albums, and was appointed a position on the National Council on Disability. Those are just some of her involvements!

Maybe God will not take you through one-tenth of that, but of this I am absolutely confident: He will give us the strength we need to do the work He has for us regardless of physical limitations!

Eighth. Do you like M&M candies? Well, there is a guaranteed step to God-confidence that is far better than the "Mmmmmm, good!" of this favorite candy. The "M&M" step to God-confidence is *memorize and meditate*. Did you notice in our chapter that each woman had a verse or several verses that gave her special strength, comfort, and encouragement to continue, to survive, and to triumph? God will do the same for you.

Select a verse, perhaps one of the verses from our chapter. Choose the verse from your favorite translation. Write it on a card. Carry it with you. Read it again and again and again until you have memorized it. Reading the verse aloud will help you to memorize it more quickly. Say the verse aloud or to yourself throughout the day. Then, whenever self-pity, doubt, and anger begin to rob you of peace and joy, say the verse to yourself and think about who God is, what He can do for you, and about each word of the verse. You will be amazed at how God will use His Word in your life on a moment-by-moment basis! Your trust in the Lord will soar! You will be comforted and strengthened faster than any pain pill or remedy ever took effect. That is the miracle-working power of God's Holy Word in your life.

Let's review the verses that our modern-day heroines have selected. Perhaps you will want to begin your personal meditation with one or all of these:

Jayni: James 1:2–3—"Consider it all joy, my brethren, when you encounter various trials, knowing that the testing of your faith produces endurance" (NASB).

Norma: Philippians 4:13—"I can do all things through Christ who strengthens me."

Sharon: Isaiah 26:3—"You will keep him in perfect peace, whose mind is stayed on You, because he trusts in You."

Jeremiah 29:11—" 'For I know the plans that I have for you,' declares the Lord, 'plans for welfare and not for calamity to give you a future and a hope' " (NASB).

1 Peter 5:7—"Casting all your care upon Him, for He cares for you."

Reflections

1. What are some of your personal health concerns?

_____

_____

_____

_____

2. How do the multiple frustrations, pain, and weariness that accompany health problems act as self-esteem destroyers for you?

_____

_____

_____

3. It has been said that "pain is inevitable, but misery is optional." Do you agree? Why, or why not?

_____

_____

_____

_____

4. What is the worst "woe of womanhood" for you? Why?

_____

_____

5. Do your health problems or those of your loved ones cause you to become frustrated or disappointed with God? Why, or why not?

_____

_____

_____

6. Of the stories shared in this chapter, which affected you most deeply? Why?

_____

_____

7. Carefully review each of the eight steps to God-confidence in the area of health concerns, and write a personal comment on each one.

_____

_____

_____

_____

_____

_____

_____

_____

8. Which verse or verses have you selected for your own personal M&M? Please write them down.

_____

_____

_____

_____

_____

_____

9. After you have committed the first verse to heart, and are beginning to think about it during the day, explain just how God is using the verse in your life.

_____

_____

_____

_____

Date of response_____

Myth Five

*God, I feel so worthless! Just when I think I am begin-
ning to learn how to trust you, and focus on you, BAM!
Something happens that fills me with those old feelings of
fear and dread, and I sink lower than ever! I'm so despon-
dent and discouraged. Why is it that I fail at almost everything I try? Why is success and accomplishment so easy
for other women?*

*Sometimes I struggle just to get through the day doing
the menial and the ordinary. When I'm around women
who seem to do everything well and have it all together, I
feel envy and want to be just like them or I panic and want
to withdraw as fast as possible. Frankly, I fear it's too late
for me to be successful. But, Father in heaven, I don't want
to believe that! Will you please do something with me, so
that my life has meaning?*

"Whatever It Is, Other Women Seem to Do It Better Than Me!"

IN MUCH OF SOUTHERN CALIFORNIA, fences and walls are used to distinguish property lines. Walls are preferred because they give an illusion of space and privacy. This is particularly significant when, in many housing tracts, the distance between the chimneys of two homes costing several hundred thousand dollars each might only be a matter of five to ten feet. The walls are also used to give a first line of defense in warding off unwelcome intruders.

During our last earthquake the much-valued boundary walls of privacy crumbled and fell. Throughout the earthquake-devastated area, there were many streets where every single block wall had toppled, revealing the yard next door. For people accustomed to the security of walls, this created great uneasiness and even fear. It was most interesting to see that many families rebuilt the outside boundary walls before repairing the inside walls.

For many of us, *accomplishments* are used to build walls of security and protection. Although much of this is unconscious, a woman feels stronger when she can say, "I'm a this," and "I do that," or "I go here," and "I'm really needed there." Being involved in outside groups and activities can also build a certain sense of security, of well-being. But when the inevitable strikes, the walls of accomplishment can crumble, leaving the inner woman revealed without the protective barrier of her outer competence.

The schools I attended never gave awards for my areas of highest achievement. I would have needed assistance in carrying the life-sized trophy I deserved for feeling *The Most Inadequate and Inferior*. Of course I was far too self-conscious and shy to have walked to the platform in my own strength to receive the trophy, anyway!

I remember with utter clarity the horror and dreadful anticipation that preceded any time I might be "called upon" to give an answer. And, in the early grades, that's a big part of the day. No wonder I hated school with a passion. Every single day reaffirmed what I already believed with all my heart and mind: *You are no good. The others are smarter. The others can do everything better than you can. No matter how hard you try you cannot catch up.* I could have been the poster girl for "Miss Lack of Self-Esteem!"

This overpowering, negative self-absorption and self-deprecation invaded every area of life. I despised the idea of "trying something new" because I knew I would be the worst at it. I abhorred the most routine form of competition, knowing I would fail. And being chosen last for every team only affirmed my worthlessness. I vividly remember many times speeding down a highway with my parents, thinking about opening the door and jumping out. But I lacked the courage.

As a young teen, I came to believe that God did love me enough to send Jesus to die for my sins. I accepted Him as my Savior, trusting that He was able to take my life and make something beautiful out of the disappointing ashes. The fact that Jesus wanted me, just as I was, astonished me. I readily gave Him my heart.

Wouldn't it be nice if we could float through life on wings of joy, soaring from one glorious mountaintop experience to another after coming to saving faith in Jesus? Well, it just ain't so. Life on earth is a training ground, a battlefield, a place for refinement, for character building. That means problems-a-plenty, just as the Bible has said, "In the world you have tribulation" (John 16:33, NASB).

Great! That's just what an insignificant, weak person like me needed to have confirmed! "In this world you have tribulation"—that was the scary part.

It took me a while to really see what follows that verse—"take courage: I have overcome the world." Thank God!

Jesus has given us, His children, a wonderful promise in Hebrews 13:5: "I will never leave you nor forsake you." Now that's the kind of news I need!

I absolutely love the comfort and vivid assurance of Isaiah 43:1-2: "Thus says the Lord, your creator, O Jacob, and He who formed you, O Israel, 'Do not fear, for I have redeemed you; I have called you by name; you are Mine! When you pass through the waters, I will be with you; and through the rivers, they will not overflow you. When you walk through the fire, you will not be scorched, nor will the flame burn you' " (NASB).

You and I have a better insurance policy than that—complete coverage through fire and flood—given to us by the omnipotent, sovereign God of the universe!

What do these words mean to us in those arduous daily treks through life? Great encouragement—if we go about the task of building our confidence in God.

As in every other area, the first barrier we need to overcome is our true, ingrained dependence on our own abilities.

Perhaps you remember that marvelous classic children's book *The Little Engine That Could*. There was a happy little train filled with all sorts of good things for boys and girls who lived on the other side of the mountain. Big problem. The engine failed. What to do. A very little engine came "chug, chugging merrily along" and kindly agreed to help. Going up the mountain was very hard with such a big load, but the Little Blue Engine cried out, "I think I can—I think I can—I think I can." On the way down the other side of the mountain the successful engine exulted, "I thought I could. I thought I could. I thought I could."[1]

Such a sweet story! How much *self* wants to believe that "I can and I will!" It is such a glorification of the self that we wish we were—competent, powerful, successful. However, real life for a Christian woman is not like that. In a prideful bubble of self-esteem I can keep parroting, "I think I can—I think I can" all day and all night, until we see the truth.

Although God can do anything, and certainly doesn't need us, He chooses to use us to accomplish His work on this earth. How utterly amazing! That means when God wants us to do something—anything—He must get us over the mountain of difficulty that is keeping us from getting it done. Charles Stanley, a nationally recognized Christian statesman, says it so well: "When God calls you to a task, He assumes the responsibility for removing those hindrances that would hinder you from accomplishing that task."[2]

Mt. Everest and Me

Teaching was a Mt. Everest difficulty for me.

The first great shock of my teaching career came the first hour of the first day of my first year. At 8:45 I walked outside to greet a third- and fourth-grade combination class composed of EMR (Educable Mentally Retarded) and EH (Emotionally Handicapped) children. I had on my best duds and my brightest smile. I was equipped with years of college, a degree, a credential that indicated I was supposedly qualified, and a lot of youthful zeal and enthusiasm! I, Pat Holt, would help these needy children. I, Pat Holt, would help them to read and write and achieve their full potential. I was in a happy bubble of self-assurance.

They were not glad to see me. I vividly remember their first words, whined almost in unison, "Where is Mrs. Kubasheck? You're not Mrs. Kubasheck!" I was thinking, *And you're lucky, too. I'm a lot nicer than she ever was or could be!* I told them she had taken the year off, and I was to be their teacher. The grumbles continued as they wandered into the classroom. My happy bubble was beginning to wiggle and waver.

In my foolish innocence and inexperience, I was certain the children would want to know my name. It could be a reading lesson. What fun! I told the class what I was going to do, then turned my back. During the ten seconds it took to write, "My name is Mrs. Holt," I heard loud shuffling and other noises that let me know I'd had it!

I had lost them, and the clock read 9:00! Recess was not until 9:45. I made an assortment of feeble attempts at gaining some modicum of control. Each failed miserably. They were in charge of the class. They knew it. I began to sweat (not glow or perspire)! The clock seemed stuck at 9:05 and would not move. I had no clue what to do. In complete panic, I checked my lesson plans. I had tried to do everything. Nothing worked, including those really hot ideas I'd saved in case I had time! TIME! That's all I had. Never, in the history of the world, including when the sun stood still, has time moved so slowly.

At 9:40, since I had already passed the point of all human endurance, I flung open the door and let the wild ones out. There were only eighteen in the class, but never has any group seemed so large, so hostile, so completely unmanageable and inhuman.

Alone, haggard and shaking, I slumped into a chair. With trembling hands clenched together, I let the Lord know, *Dear God, I hate this class! I can't stand them for an hour, much less a year! How could you let this happen to me, your child, who is simply doing your will?*

Somehow I survived the rest of the day. I don't know how. It is a complete blur. I have no recollection of what happened, except to know that I had never felt so publicly defeated and so physically wrung out.

Driving home through a torrent of tears, I pulled to the side and wept and wept. I demanded of God, "Why? Why? Why did you let me waste all those years in college and then go into something where you knew I was going to be a failure? Why do you want me to be a failure and a disgrace? Everyone knows I'm a Christian. Why did you let everyone see how out of control my children were, and hear them screaming and yelling everywhere they went?

Why didn't you protect me? You could have given me a nice class my first year. Why didn't you?" On and on my shameful tantrum went, until I was too exhausted to rant and rave anymore.

After all the tears were gone and all that remained were the choking gasps, I quieted down and uttered a single word: "Help!" That was the first step—asking the Lord for help. I confessed to Him, "God, I can't do it. You know it, I know it, and every teacher in the school knows it! Dear God, I really believe you wanted me to be a teacher. If that's true, then take me, and make me into your teacher—please!"

I didn't know what He could do or would do, if anything. I didn't know how He could help me tame the wild ones in my class, but He was the only one I could go to and talk to about my being a hopeless failure.

In the days and nights that followed, I prayed continually to the Lord, pleading with Him to help me somehow, someway. During one of these prayer sessions the Lord brought to my mind and heart James 1:5: "If any of you lacks wisdom, let him ask of God, who gives to all men liberally and without reproach, and it will be given to him."

That was the second step—asking the Lord for wisdom. I asked the Lord to make that verse a reality in my life in relation to my class. I had no idea how to handle them. Sure, I'd had all the courses and had observed and done student teaching. But so what? All that head knowledge was not helping one little bit. The children in my class were so young, and yet so hard and experienced and worldly wise. How could I break through? What techniques could possibly work with these children? Which techniques for which child?

And then, as I began to ask the Lord for wisdom, He showed me that I needed something more to reach those kids—something that He alone could give me that would change my attitude and the attitude and behavior of the kids. Along with the wisdom to know how to discipline them, I needed to know how to reach them, to hang on to them. And for that I needed to *love* them.

That was the third step—asking the Lord for love. A hard one. I didn't really want to love them, but then the Lord reminded me, "My Son died to save the children in your class." That was a terrible moment of revelation for me. Christ loved these children: I hated them. After some gulps and tears, I asked the Lord to give me love for these unlovely children—children who were viewed as the garbage of the school district and the bane of their parents' existence.

Lessons From the School of Hard Knocks

Slowly, ever so slowly it seemed to me, the Lord began to work in my heart and life first, changing my attitudes and my thinking patterns, and then—finally—with the children themselves.

The first few months were pretty horrible. Chairs were thrown at me. A switchblade was waved in my face. The profusion of filthy words, obscene gestures, and bizarre behavior went on and on. But even in those precarious circumstances—for which I was *never* prepared in college—the Lord was faithful as He promised. I could feel Him giving me the patience and the calming, authoritative words to speak. The same God that was with David when he killed Goliath, the same God that was with Daniel in the lions' den—I knew He was with me in my time of fear and testing.

By January my class was transformed. In fact, it became the hit of the district. It was the model special-education class for miles around. There wasn't a week that went by that I didn't have at least two or three observers— college students, supervisors, and teachers from my district or other districts who came to see what a successful special class was like, to ask questions, and to ask for help and advice. And the Lord gave me the wisdom, ideas, and words as I shared with these people. They were amazed at my control, at my love for the children, and the children's respect and love for me as well as their desire to cooperate.

By the last day of school in June, some of the children even cried when they left. They didn't want school to ever end—not with their home lives! They wanted the peace, the security, the fun and happiness that their haven of a classroom represented. Who could blame them? It had really become the Lord's Special-Education class!

Many years have gone by. Because of what the Lord taught me that first fateful year, I have never had a serious discipline problem again. In fact, all who know me would tell you immediately that "discipline" is probably my greatest area of strength and expertise. Why? Because I was tutored by God. My Savior and Lord took my enormous mountain of weakness and transformed it into an area of superior strength. Yes, out of my weakness came His strength. I would not trade that experience for anything.

Because it was God's will for me to be a teacher, He equipped me to do that work for Him after I yielded (albeit reluctantly) in submission to Him. He certainly didn't do it my way or in my time frame. He did it His way, in the way that brought honor and glory to His name, and in the way that gave my God-confidence a huge leap forward.

It is just marvelous to see how God works. He takes a weak woman, like me, totally lacking in self-esteem and gives her a mountainous task too hard to do, so that she is further humbled—convinced she cannot do it. Then she yields, gives up—only to see how beautifully God accomplishes the task in and through her. When facing any of life's many, many mountains, how I love Zechariah 4:6: " 'Not by might, nor by power, but by my Spirit,' says the Lord of hosts."

Pat

For many women, the experiences of early years form towering mountains of worthlessness. Humanly speaking, they are insurmountable obstacles, guaranteed to obliterate any "self-esteem." But then God takes the overpowering weakness, and creates the beauty and the strength.

Pat Mac is a very bright, highly competent, quick-witted woman with a wonderful smile and an infectious laugh. But she was not always this way—not by a long shot. She was raised in a home with a domineering father who wasted no opportunity to reinforce her feelings of worthlessness. "You are stupid!" were the words imprinted on her mind from the beginning. Her mother was totally subservient, and too afraid of her father to be of comfort.

Her grandfather was a minister, so she was allowed to attend church. "Because my exposure to God came at such a young age, I always had that quiet security within me. I was always talking to Jesus—always—for as long as I remember."

Pat was not allowed to play with other children. Going to school meant more problems. "I was amazed by the behavior of my classmates. They had freedom to express themselves verbally. At home, I was not allowed to talk unless I was spoken to." Already painfully shy, Pat reacted by becoming more withdrawn. She stayed to herself unless approached. The very idea of getting up in front of the class was devastating.

In junior high, Pat moved. "This was hard. I was removed from my grandmother, who was my only human source of encouragement. I was an early developer, was ashamed, and became even more socially withdrawn."

The downhill side of inferiority continued. "In school I thought I could not do the work. I always did it, but I had no confidence. I never had any help at home. It was 'my job.' It was futile to discuss my work. If I couldn't do it I would hear, as I did so often, 'You are stupid!' Although my grades were not good, I was given a job in the high school office. I was always relied upon and trusted. When I was fifteen, I remember looking at my test scores. They indicated I was a level above a moron. This corroborated what my father had told me for years, and what I believed was true. But even at that point, I still would talk to Jesus any time, any place, believing that in Jesus there was no criticism, no judgment. I always believed that Jesus loved me unconditionally. Jesus was always my best friend."

Pat had neither the desire nor the grades for college. Her father insisted she try junior college. "I flunked out and got a job." She became so encouraged at her new job that she went to business trade school and did well.

What kept her going despite her learning disabilities? "Jesus was my constant support. Even though I was constantly trying to fit into a square of acceptability but never could fit the pattern, Jesus gave me the strength to persevere. God was always there. I never equated my father with God. Nothing and no one could ever touch my relationship with God. It was my support. The light never went out."

Belinda

Belinda is a petite brunette, with a pretty turned-up nose, a rosebud mouth, and a beautiful singing voice. A fragile, vulnerable quality surrounds her. I wasn't certain she would want to discuss her childhood. "If what I have been through can help even one person, it will have been worth it," was her reply.

Her parents divorced early. "But Dad came and went through the years, like the wind. I never knew when he'd be there and when he wouldn't. Of course I believed the divorce was my fault."

Times were hard. Belinda's mom was a waitress, and her father didn't live up to his alimony payments. There was a terrible financial strain. "I was made fun of because of the clothes I wore, the trailer we lived in, and the way we lived. I was picked on a lot because I was small. I remember many tears. I tried to stay out of people's way and never draw attention to myself."

Alcohol dictated the family's lifestyle. "Everybody drank," Belinda recalls. "My grandma drank to get drunk. Because she didn't like the taste of whiskey, she would gulp it down with a beer chaser. My mom, dad, and grandma could drink for days at a time."

"I never knew how I was going to be treated. It all depended. I remember changing the television channel when Dad was watching something. He went into a tirade. I turned it back too late. He slammed the door and went to the bar down the street. Mom took me with her later to find him. He wasn't there. She slugged me and screeched, 'It's all your fault! If you wouldn't have changed channels, he wouldn't have left.'

"You just never knew what would happen. Dad would yell and beat Mom. One time she retaliated by burning his clothes. Then he smashed the headlights of the car and shattered the front door.

"Mom would go out on dates when Dad wasn't there, and not come home. My brother and I were left alone. I remember being afraid a lot. I never knew what to expect.

"I remember when Grandma was at our house and so drunk she couldn't drive. But she wanted to get to the liquor store. I was so afraid something would happen to her. I got in the car and did the shifting so she could get there safely.

"When I was in third grade, Mom and Dad were screaming at each other again. Mom mixed up some lye and threatened, 'If you leave, I'm drinking this!' He left and she drank some. She was in the hospital for what seemed like months. Her body never recovered.

"During summer vacation of that year, a woman in the neighborhood picked up some children and took us to Vacation Bible School. I had no knowledge of the Lord prior to this. I remember the story and the song about the Wordless Book. I asked Jesus to come into my heart. For two years I attended a Good News Club in her trailer once a week. It was here that I learned some spiritual survival skills. I'll never forget those times. It helped me when my mom taunted me with a knife, threatening to slit her wrists because 'It's all your fault!' It didn't matter what it was; I just knew it was all my fault.

"I can never get away from the memories. My experience has made me what I am. I am certain that if I had not come to know the Lord I would be an alcoholic today!"

I asked Belinda how she survives today. "I don't blame anyone. You can't wallow and make excuses. As soon as you get into self-pity, Satan has you. I encourage myself with God's Word. The verses that got me through then and get me through now are Proverbs 3:5–6: 'Trust in the Lord with all your heart, and lean not on your own understanding; In all your ways acknowledge Him, and He shall direct your paths.' Romans 8:28 is my other favorite. 'And we know that all things work together for good to those who love God, to those who are called according to His purpose.' Did you notice? It doesn't say it will be good. But it does say that He will work whatever it is out for good. I believe that. I've seen it happen in my life, and in other people's lives."

It has been well said that "life can be counted on to provide all the pain that any of us might need."[3] It is the way that God takes the pain of our lives and makes us stronger that fashions us into women of God-confidence.

Candice

Candice wanted to be on the drill team. Her dream began in sixth grade and continued through junior high and into high school. It was all that really mattered. Everything else seemed insignificant in comparison.

She was never good at sports. "P.E. was a nightmare," Candice relates. "Every day I dreaded P.E. because I couldn't do any of the sports and didn't like them. People would make fun of me, and get mad at me because I would make the team lose. This happened as far back as I can remember."

Although Candice worked for two years to get ready for the drill team tryouts, she didn't make it. "I was devastated. I felt that all my hopes and dreams had crashed around my feet when I didn't make it. Sounds stupid, I know, but that's the way it was. Of course my best friend made the team, which made my rejection that much more painful.

"I began to question the Lord and doubt everything I'd known before. I reasoned, 'How can He really love me when He doesn't give me the only thing I really want?' I'd even prayed about it."

But God did not give up on Candice. "A few months later in P.E., we had to run the mile. We had never done much running before. I was one of the only ones who had the stamina to complete the mile, even though I was slow. I probably had the stamina because of all my working out for the drill team!

"The cross-country coaches asked me if I wanted to join the team. I did not want to at first. I'd never really been good at anything, and I didn't want to try and fail. It seemed too hard anyway. My parents encouraged me to join. After a while I thought, 'Why not? I can always quit if it doesn't work out.' "

Candice was in cross country for four years, and loved every day of it, although she never became fast. "In fact, I was always one of the slowest."

She learned three important lessons for later life. "First, I learned that God is who He said He is, and that He is faithful. Because cross country is so hard, physically, my strength would just leave me in the middle of the three-mile races up and down hills. I would cry out to God, and He would help me get through. I would think Isaiah 40:31 as I ran: 'But those who wait on the Lord shall renew their strength. They shall mount up with wings like eagles. They shall run and not be weary. They shall walk and not faint.'

"I also learned that there was something more important than being the best, or even being really good. I learned that I just had to do my best before God. The other thing I learned was the importance of serving others. Even though I wasn't good, I could help other people excel by encouraging them."

Candice is my twenty-year-old daughter, and I must add a mother's note: She was selected by her fellow team members as the *Most Inspirational Player* for both her eleventh- and twelfth-grade years. Truly, God took her dream for success and molded it into something far better for himself, for others, and for her. Out of devastated "self-esteem" is growing a woman whose confidence is in God.

A Higher View

These are tough lessons for some of us to accept, in a world that incessantly shouts, "Successful people are the ones with the outstanding accomplishments." God's idea of "success" is vastly different than the world's. Most of God's success stories will not be revealed until we get to heaven and our eyes are finally, fully opened to life from a higher view.

Mazie is a woman with one of these stories. You've never heard of her, and you never will on this earth. While here, she referred to herself in later years as "a trophy of God's grace."

She was a housekeeper to the stars. Her husband was a chauffeur. Although they could not participate in the affluent lifestyles of their famous employers, they did learn to drink—a lot! Their jobs were important to them, too important for children. She learned to perform her own abortions. Her "miracle child" survived her best abortion efforts.

Later Mazie and her husband came to know Jesus. The abuses to her body caused severe heart problems, and she tired more and more easily. What could she do? How could she serve the Lord who had rescued her from the pit? Mazie knew how to pray, and believed that "the effective, fervent prayer of a righteous man [or woman] avails much" (James 5:16). Mazie delighted in praying for others. Even as she was confined to her home and to her bed, she prayed . . . and prayed . . . and prayed! That was her ministry, her "only" ministry. Changing lives through prayer. Literally hundreds of lives were touched because of the prayers of an invalid ex-housekeeper who "did nothing but pray."

When we all get to heaven, there will be many surprises. Of that I am confident. Some Christian women have had the applause and recognition of others here on earth. They can speak better, sing better, and perform better at all levels than most of us. And that's OK, you and I don't have to be "the best," according to human standards. We must be God's best for us, and He bears the responsibility of showing us what that means and how to do it as we trust and obey.

When you and I become God-confident enough to "just" do God's will for us, we will be rescued from such "self-esteem" lies as, "I have to be as good she is at (whatever)." No you don't, and no I don't! God never puts on us the pressure to conform to other people. We do that to ourselves, and our enemy is there to encourage us to do it. In God's Word, He says "when they measure themselves by themselves, and compare themselves with themselves, they are without understanding" (2 Corinthians 10:12, NASB). Whew! I'm so thankful. That is so comforting, reassuring, and encouraging to anyone who has ever suffered with *comparisonitis*!

No "Failure" Moms

In the arena of "accomplishments," we have to address motherhood.

I spend a great deal of my life talking to women who are mothers, and observing them in action with their children—kids they love and would give their lives for in an instant. When a mom is having an obvious child-rearing problem with a young child, one of two things generally happens. She either excuses and defends what her child is doing (if she can't possibly ignore it), or she handles the specific problem on the spot. Incidentally, this often means removing the child from the situation and dealing with the child in private.

Which do you think takes the most confidence? Dealing with the situation, of course. A mom who is struggling with her own feelings of helplessness and worthlessness will have a tougher time feeling confident in parenting.

I have witnessed the most marvelous transformations in a mom as she discovers more about who God is and what He wants to do for her personally and as a mother. I have observed that a mom's ability to deal with parenting issues rises in direct proportion to her increase in God-confidence. Sure, there are always problems related to parenting. But what job do you know that doesn't present challenges?

As the years go by, the problems can become more severe, particularly if the mom was ineffectual in dealing with the child in the early years. These problems are heartbreaking in the extreme and certainly destroy any self-esteem that might be left over in the parenting department.

One mom I've known for more than twenty years told me recently, "I wish I were dead!" Her fifteen-year-old daughter was pregnant by one of two or three suitors. Dealing with her teenager has become as difficult as harnessing a runaway train. "I have hit bottom," she wept. "Our life is a living hell. I am a complete and utter failure as a mother."

Her only encouragement right now is to know that God has not given up on her, her family, or her daughter. Frankly, it would be fairly easy for my friend to look back through the years and enumerate the things that led up to this moment. To what point? Most moms who experience this type of devastation know some of what should or could have been done differently. And even the most diligent of us have our regrets, don't we?

But God is with her. In her sorrow this woman said in a quivering voice, "My only comfort is to know that 'God is our refuge and strength, a very present help in trouble' (Psalm 46:1), and to know that 'the Lord is my light and my salvation' " (Psalm 27:1, KJV).

Ruth Bell Graham understands *Prodigals and Those Who Love Them*. In her poignant poem, "She Waited for the Call That Never Came," Mrs. Graham captures the aching heart of a grieving mom.

> She waited for the call
> that never came;
> searched every mail
> for a letter,
> or a note,
> or a card
> that bore his name;
> and on her knees
> at night,
> and on her feet
> all day,
> she stormed Heaven's gate
> in his behalf;
> she pled for him
> in Heaven's high court.
> "Be still, and wait, and see"—
> the word God gave;
> then she
> knew that He would
> do in and for and with him
> that which she never could.
> So doubts ignored
> she went about her chores
> with you—
> knowing though spurned,
> His word was true.
> The prodigal had not returned,
> but God was God,
> and there was work to do.[4]

Yes, God is God and God knows. God hears. God understands. God will be there with us when we go through the fiery trials, whatever they may be. Although our personal esteem is a pile of ashes, our God-confidence will grow. Like Shadrach, Meshach, and Abednego, we can emerge from the furnace of affliction stronger and more confident than when we entered.

Steps to God-confidence in Our Accomplishments

First, ask Him to either deliver you from the self-centered desire to achieve, to succeed, to excel, and to teach you how to achieve His goals in His way.

Second, realize that God chooses to humble us of self-esteem so that we will learn to trust Him. Then He can use us for the purposes He intends.

Hannah Hurnard is a well-known Christian author. One of her best known and best loved books is entitled *Hinds' Feet on High Places*, and is an allegory dramatizing the journey each of us must take before we can live in the "high places." Habakkuk 3:19 is central to the story: "The Lord God is my strength, and he will make my feet like hinds' feet, and he will make me to walk upon mine high places" (KJV).

The humblings of her early life well prepared her to write about the Lord being her strength:

"I was a miserable, morbid, self-centered person who never felt love for anyone, shut up to my own torment. Till I was nineteen I never remember feeling happy, though of course I sometimes stopped feeling unhappy. I had two hateful and tormenting handicaps. One, a horrible stammer, which, whenever I tried to speak, kept me mouthing in a desperate effort to get the words out. Until I was nineteen, I never went into a shop alone, nor onto a bus or train, or anywhere where I might be obliged to speak. As a child, when we were playing in the garden alone and I was natural and unselfconscious, I could often say whole sentences, but if spoken to or asked a question the ghastly struggles began at once.

"I simply hated people—the unfeeling ones and even the kind ones who looked away and were horribly sorry and embarrassed. At school I suffered torments and appeared a perfect fool, always saying I didn't know the answers to questions because I couldn't get the answers out.

"The other handicap was, in some ways, even worse than the stammer. I was obsessed by tormenting fears, some quite ordinary ones such as many other people share, but also many abnormal ones, at least perhaps I experienced them to an abnormal degree and more or less continuously. I felt terror of the dark, terror of heights, a maddening terror of being shut in anywhere, terror of crowds, of being ill and of fainting and losing consciousness, and above all, a daily and nightly experienced horror of death.

"The older I grew, the more I felt the humiliation and hurt of my stammer. Morning after morning I awoke feeling that I simply could not face another day. I longed for the courage to commit suicide. Thus I grew more and more morbid and tormented and shut up to myself, unable to think of anything but my own unspeakable wretchedness.

"All this time, though I would have given anything to believe that there was a God who could help even me, He seemed to take no notice, to pay no attention to my despairing prayers and to become more and more unreal and inaccessible.

"Why do I emphasize all this? Because in one half hour, when I was nineteen years of age, my whole life was changed and this hateful, abnormal husk split and fell off and left me, not with a new physical make up or another mental outfit but with an absolutely transformed outlook."[5]

When Hannah Hurnard met Jesus, an amazing transformation took place. But our Sovereign God knew that her early struggles would infuse depth and sensitivity to the writing He planned for her to do. As a result, many thousands of women have been blessed through the years.

Third, never forget that "when I am weak, then I am strong" through His power and strength (2 Corinthians 12:10). You and I will be able to do what God intends.

Those high mountains of things that seem impossible to overcome really do become opportunities for God to demonstrate His overcoming power.

God delights in choosing the weak things of the world to show His strength (1 Corinthians 1:27). He did it all through His Word and He will do it with you.

Gladys Aylward was a poor candidate for becoming a missionary. Her lack of academic ability, even at the age of twenty-eight, caused her to be rejected by the China Inland Mission Training School. She was advised to do something "more suited to your abilities," which meant continuing domestic work. Gladys cringed. She believed God wanted her to be a missionary to China. But how? No mission board would send her. In her simple, profound faith she believed God would send her. And He did. She worked as a domestic in London, saving every penny she could to give the ticket master, who held her dreams of China in his hand.

Two years later she had enough money to finish paying for a one-way third-class ticket on the Trans-Siberian Express.

Curiously enough, mastering the Chinese language was no problem for Gladys. She quickly learned it by mimicking the Chinese. Something she never could have done with a book. Gladys was a masterful storyteller. God had given her the innate ability to share the gospel with captivating and highly dramatic Bible stories.

Her life was full of daring journeys and adventures, which have been recounted in several biographies and the film *Inn of the Sixth Happiness*.

One of her most incredible escapades involved fleeing for over one month during the Chinese-Japanese War to one of Madame Chiang Kai-shek's orphanages over the mountains. With almost no provisions, on foot, and with more than one hundred children ranging in age from three to sixteen, and only one adult assistant, she led the group to safety in Free China. The extraordinary journey paralleled her favorite Bible story of the Israelites' deliverance from Egypt.

"During the harrowing journey, she grappled with despair as never before. After passing a sleepless night, she faced the morning with no hope of reaching safety. A thirteen-year-old girl in the group reminded her of their much loved story of Moses and the Israelites crossing the Red Sea.

" 'But I am not Moses,' Gladys cried in desperation.

" 'Of course you are not,' the girl said, 'but Jehovah is still God!' "[6]

Fourth, ask the Lord to deliver you from impossible human expectations and from the curse of "comparisonitis." You are totally unique and different from anyone who has ever lived. There will never again be anyone just like you, and no one but you can do what God intends for you to do.

Maybe you will become a famous author like Hannah Hurnard, or have thrilling adventures like Gladys Aylward. But it really doesn't matter. All that matters is doing God's will for you in God's way and leaving the results to Him.

Perhaps there is some simple thing in your life that you think you should be able to do, like arts and crafts was for me. Something that you think you should be able to do well because all the "other girls are doing it." Go to the Lord about it and seek His will. In Jeremiah 29:13 He promises that "you will seek Me and find Me, when you search for Me with all your heart." God *will* reveal His will to you. He will either teach you how to do it, as He did for me with discipline, or He will free you from the bondage of thinking you have to be good at whatever it is.

Remember also, God does *not* play "hide-and-seek" to keep us guessing and wondering in anxiety just what on earth He wants. As you seek to do His will, He will reveal it. That's because He loves you and wants to lead and guide you in the way that He knows is best for you.

Fifth, trust the Lord to make changes in your attitude and also your performance.

It seems as though "everyone" is making bread. So I

thought I, too, would become the happy little homemaker producing fresh loaves of bread daily. What fun! Breathes there a woman who does not envision a kitchen smelling like fresh baked bread?

The first step was to purchase the right bread-making machine. I had already been an abysmal failure with my feeble attempts at traditional bread-making. My loaves could either double as doorstops, or did not rise above the level of the ingredients!

After the purchase, the serious baking began in earnest. I honestly believed that any fool could be a successful bread-maker with the proper machine! WRONG! I spent more time dialing the "Bread Hot Line" number than I did in the kitchen. I figured it had to be the machine. After all, I knew of small children that were baking beautiful loaves of bread.

A new, improved turbo model entered the house. I was really determined. I was desperate for success in this area of homemaking. Well, for every edible loaf, my family endured two or three failures. But they were encouraging, knowing how much this meant to me.

My husband also gave me subtle encouragement. Besides eating the bread no matter how dry—or moist—it was, he purchased a bread-making cookbook for me that had a lot of tips for "new bakers."

Of course I wanted to please, so I flipped through the pages marking recipes to try. In my heart I was ready to give up, but thought I'd give the Sunflower Bread a try. I assembled the ingredients, diligently following the recipe. To my utter delight, it rose beautifully and smelled great.

Dave cut some to eat in the van pool on the way to work. Bad idea! But he is such a man of faith and hope. After one chewy bite he made the discovery: There were sunflower shells, as well as seeds, permeating the entire loaf. He spent the long trip to the office picking through the bread, looking for places to discard the itsy-bitsy pieces of shells. Funny thing—none of the other riders ever asked for my recipe.

Still not wanting to discourage me, the family compared notes at dinner. Each had a similar experience and kindly suggested, "You might want to purchase sunflower seeds without shells the next time you bake this type of bread!"

That did it. I recalled I had never prayed about my bread baking. So I began to pray and ask Him either to deliver me from the desire to bake bread or teach me how to do it. Well, He is teaching me how. I'll never be "the best," but I'm having better loaves than before and a lot less waste!

Mrs. James Garfield, wife of President James Garfield, also had trouble with bread. Skill wasn't her problem. Attitude was. She preferred literary and cultural interests to domestic duties.

However, she learned an important lesson about attitude many years before she became First Lady. Making great batches of bread appeared to be an inescapable duty, so she determined that she would overcome her dislike for this chore by taking a very special interest in it. She wrote:

> The whole of life became brighter. The very sunshine seemed to be flowing down through my spirit into the white loaves, and now I believe my table is furnished with better bread than ever before: and this truth, as old as creation, seems just now to have become fully mine—that I need not be the shrinking slave of toil, but its regal master.[7]

Sixth, focus on applying Colossians 3:23 on a moment-by-moment basis: "Whatever [and that means everything from cleaning a toilet to running a business] you do, do it heartily, as to the Lord and not to men [and that includes women]."

This relieves the stress of being like everybody else, as good as "them," or of even having to do what "they" are doing, or doing it the way "they" are doing it, or even doing it when "they" are doing it!

You do not have to succumb to people pressure. Very

often, it is a choice women make when feeling particularly ineffective and insecure. Focusing on God and His Word will relieve you of the overpowering anxiety and stress of people pressure.

As God-confidence increases, people pressure decreases. When God is the center the competition ends. And with it, envy and jealousy die. The result? the peace and freedom to be just who God wants you to be . . . and nobody else.

Ron Mehl has written an excellent book entitled *Surprise Endings*. In it he gives this sound bit of advice:

> People get into trouble when they try to be more, do more, and have more than God has designed. They flippantly quote Philippians 4:13, "I can do all things through Christ who strengthens me." It's a great truth, but so often misapplied. Some believe it to mean you can do anything you want to do, be anything you want to be, go anywhere you want to go. I don't believe that's what Paul is saying. I think he's saying that with the help and strength of Jesus Christ I'll go where He wants me to go, be what He wants me to be, and do what He wants me to do. I once heard my mentor, Jack Hayford, say, "Without Him, we cannot. Without us, He will not."[8]

Seventh—M&M. Remember, that means *Memorize and Meditate!*

To keep your mind from drawing a zero during your times of greatest need, you must have His Word in your memory bank.

Let's review the key verses from the women in this chapter:

Pat: James 1:5—"If any of you lacks wisdom, let him [or her] ask God, who gives to all men [women too!] generously and without reproaching, and it will be given him [and her]" (RSV).

Zechariah 4:6—"Not by might, nor by power, but by my

spirit, saith the Lord of hosts." (KJV)

Belinda: Proverbs 3:5–6—"Trust in the Lord with all your heart, and lean not on your own understanding; in all your ways acknowledge Him, and He shall direct your paths."

Romans 8:28—"And we know that all things work together for good to those who love God, to those who are the called according to His purpose."

Candice: Isaiah 40:31—"But those who wait on the LORD shall renew their strength; they shall mount up with wings like eagles, they shall run and not be weary, they shall walk and not faint."

Mazie: James 5:16—"The effective, fervent prayer of a righteous man [or woman] avails much."

A grieving mom: Psalm 46:1—"God is our refuge and strength, a very present help in trouble" (KJV).

A grieving mom: Psalm 27:1—"The LORD is my light and my salvation."

Hannah Hurnard: Habakkuk 3:19—"The Lord God is my strength, and he will make my feet like hinds' feet, and he will make me to walk upon mine high places" (KJV).

Each woman: 2 Corinthians 12:10—"When I am weak, then I am strong."

2 Corinthians 10:12—"When they measure themselves by themselves, and compare themselves with themselves, they are without understanding" (NASB).

1 Corinthians 1:27—"And God has chosen the weak things of the world to put to shame the things which are mighty."

Jeremiah 29:13—"You will seek Me and find Me, when you search for Me with all your heart" (NASB)

Colossians 3:23—"Whatever you do, do it heartily, as to the Lord and not to men."

Reflections

1. In which three areas of your life does lack of accomplishment, or "not measuring up," cause you the most frustration?

_____

_____

_____

2. What were the most significant hurts/humiliations in your early life?

_____

_____

_____

3. Charles Stanley has said, "In everything God allows in our lives, we must look for His fingerprint." How have you seen the fingerprint of God working in and through your feelings of worthlessness?

_____

_____

_____

4. Which story in this chapter came the closest to identifying with your situation? Why?

_____

_____

_____

5. In thinking about "comparisonitis," in which areas of accomplishment are you most likely to compare yourself with other women? Please be specific.

_____

_____

_____

6. What are you going to do to avoid leading a people-pressured life in the future?

_____

_____

_____

7. Carefully review each of the seven steps to God-confidence in the area of accomplishments and write a personal comment on each one.

_____

_____

_____

_____

_____

_____

_____

8. Select one or more verses for your own personal "M&M." Write them down.

_____

_____

_____

_____

_____

9. After you have committed the first verse to memory, and are beginning to think about it during the day, explain how God is using it in your life.

_____

_____

_____

_____

Date of response_____

Myth Six

Dear Lord, sometimes my desire for possessions appalls me. Why is it that I long for all the things that money can buy? Why is it that when I spend and get, I feel more important and more secure? But that feeling leaves so fast, and I need something newer, something better in order to keep feeling like I'm significant.

And why do I care so much about keeping up with other people? In comparison, I sometimes feel like a kid huddled outside a great window in the cold night air, looking in to see how the other side lives. I know this is wrong, and I don't like being this way. You are doing so much in my life already—but in this area, my desires can get out of control. Please help me get a grip on the reality of your will! Thank you, Father God.

"No Matter What I Have, 'They' Always Have More!"

MY MOTHER IS CERTAIN it all started before I was two. According to her, I toddled into her room and headed straight for the fine jewelry. Adorning my chubby fingers with her wedding and engagement rings, I then wobbled to the living room sofa, where I got comfortable and admired the look of my newly acquired treasures. Weary from the effort, I fell asleep with my hands stretched out, displaying the finery.

Yes, it's true. I've always had a predilection for all the lovelies that life has to offer! As a little girl I watched with wonder as the glamorous Ginger Rogers and debonair Fred Astaire danced across the lavish stage with elegance and grace. Surely this was a representation of life as it should be lived!

My mother was my role model, and was the mistress par excellence of shopping and spending. I wanted to be just like Mom.

Because of my father's elevated position in Los Angeles City Government, there were perks-a-plenty! Front and center is where we always sat. From our enviable and nearly unattainable box seats at the Hollywood Bowl, I turned to look at the sea of faces in the distance—those people in the cheap seats.

On our yearly jaunts to Europe, the limos were in waiting to smoothly glide us to deluxe suites in world-renowned hotels. Private sightseeing tours with limo driver and guide alternated with fine dining in fashionable establishments. Naturally, shopping sprees were an important part of the European experience.

Curiously, I never thought about words like "waste" and "indulgence" as a girl. This was just the way life was, and it got better all the time.

Isn't it interesting that the same girl who lived like this was painfully shy, had zero self-esteem, and felt completely inferior in every way? Of course, I never made the connection.

Enter Dave

With my parents' complete approval, I married Dave, a man of humble origin, who worked hard—and who simply loved the Lord with all his heart, mind, and soul, and esteemed his wife far better than himself. But rude awakenings lay in wait.

Our income was no match for *my* lifestyle! What a dilemma! There had to be a way, and I was not about to sacrifice my lifestyle!

The designer dress sketched in the L.A. *Times* took nearly a page. I loved it at first sight and wanted it. The thought swiftly crossed my mind: *You can't afford it!* Another thought, a much stronger and more insistent thought countered, *But I want it and I'm going to have it!* How?

Then I remembered the little plastic cards my mother always used—so much simpler than carrying around cash. What was good enough for Mom was good enough for me in my hour of need.

I got that first card so quickly and easily, purchased the dress, and glided away in an excited rush of excitement! What fun! I felt so good. I felt so very grown up! I was doing what I'd learned from Mom, but doing it all by myself. I had such a great time that I used that card again and *again* and *again*. The adrenaline flowed with the ecstasy of shopping and spending. I had never felt more in control. I was on my way to credit-card heaven.

The bill at the end of the month was a momentary

downer, but there was some good news! I didn't need to pay it all. I just had to give the store a little bit. No big deal. I was so encouraged.

What I refused to consider was that my mother always paid off each credit card at the end of every month. She spent, but she could afford it. I couldn't.

If one bit of plastic was good, then more pieces of plastic were better. Plastic meant power! The more plastic I had, the more powerful I felt. Yes, for those delightful spending moments in time, I had "self-esteem," and I liked it—a lot! In terms of defending my spending, I would laugh and say, "I'm in training for streets of gold!"

Unfortunately, those end-of-the-month "minimum payments" were getting larger all the time. Soon they were too large. Reality was interfering with my plans! A possible solution: Get more money. Well, that didn't seem to be an option. The answer came in a flash of inspiration—GET MORE CARDS!

The cycle continued. I got a thrill of excitement, a "rush," a pounding of adrenaline flowing through my body from shopping and spending that was unparalleled. Does this sound like addiction? Well, as any ex-addict knows, you first deceive yourself. "I can handle it. I've got it under control. It's OK." The addict does anything and everything to protect the "feel-good feelings" that come with the addiction.

What about God? God was there. God is always there. His Holy Spirit was convicting me of my sin against Him, against my husband, against my family, against all those others I could have been helping if I hadn't been so heavily in debt.

The Lord used my children's education as the way of jolting me into coming to terms with my addiction. Private education is expensive. There was no way to continue my spending habits and be able to afford the schools into which the Lord was leading them.

I know now that I will always be in danger of becoming a shopping and spending addict again—and that I must

123

rely on the power of God to control my addiction, asking Him to take over and be the control of my finances. It is a burden I cannot bear. I failed miserably and succumbed to the temptations and foolish allures of the world system.

Frankly, I have often wondered why God has not stripped me of every penny I ever had or would have. It certainly is what I deserve. But in spite of my guilt and shame, I accept His grace to deliver me and His mercy to forgive me, thanking Him for not giving up on His self-indulgent child.

The verses that have meant so much to me in dealing with my weakness are found in 2 Corinthians 10:4–5: "For the weapons of our warfare are not carnal but mighty in God for pulling down strongholds, casting down arguments and every high thing that exalts itself against the knowledge of God, bringing every thought into captivity to the obedience of Christ."

Although the shopping and spending sprees gave me momentary feelings of power, control, and worth, the results sank me deeper into the pit of despair and worthlessness. God-confidence in this area has come as a direct result of giving up self-will, yielding to His will, and trusting Him for His control and direction.

"This I recall to my mind, therefore I have hope. Through the Lord's mercies we are not consumed, because His compassions fail not. They are new every morning; great is Your faithfulness. 'The Lord is my portion,' says my soul, 'therefore I hope in Him!' " These verses from Lamentations 3:21–24 have encouraged and sustained me a multitude of times.

Just about the time God was dealing with me in this area, friends asked Dave and me to go to the Hollywood Bowl with them. They had the tickets. We were their guests. It had been years since I'd been to the Bowl, and I eagerly looked forward to the evening.

When we got there, we kept walking and walking, higher and higher. I thought I'd get a nosebleed! Our seats were nearly in the very back row! Of course it had never occurred to me to bring binoculars! I had to smile, and you know why? Because it didn't matter! It really didn't matter! I was so thrilled with that realization. I didn't have to sit in the "right" box with the "right" people, dining on an elegant picnic menu! I was amazed at what God was doing in my life. The Almighty God of the universe was giving me—nothing of Pat Holt on her own—His confidence! I was becoming a miracle of God's grace. My God-confidence took another gigantic boost forward!

Obviously, I am a kindergartner in God's school of fiscal responsibility! (But watch out! I'm getting ready for first grade really fast!) My story is simple compared with many. But God's principles are the same, and apply from kindergarten through graduate school!

Celebration of Discipline

In his book *Celebration of Discipline* Richard Foster states:

> Inwardly, modern man is fractured and fragmented. He is trapped in a maze of competing attachments. One moment he makes decision on the basis of sound reason and the next moment out of fear of what others will think of him. He has no unity or focus around which his life is oriented.
>
> Because we lack a divine Center, our need for security has led us into an insane attachment to things. We must clearly understand that the lust for affluence in contemporary society is psychotic. It is psychotic because it has completely lost touch with reality. We crave things we neither need nor enjoy. "We buy things we do not want to impress people we do not like." Where planned obsolescence leaves off, psychological obsolescence takes over. We are made to feel ashamed to wear clothes or drive cars until they are worn out. The mass media have convinced us that to be out of step with fashion is to be out of step with reality. It is time we awaken to the fact that conformity to a sick

society is to be sick. Until we see how unbalanced our culture has become at this point we will not be able to deal with the mammon spirit within ourselves nor will we desire Christian simplicity.[1]

Beverly desperately wanted to keep up with "them." She strained and stretched, charged and borrowed, in a futile attempt to purchase acceptability with the people she wanted to be her friends. Although she never really felt comfortable with "them," it was still her goal and the longing of her heart to be like them. She rationalized: "Most of these people don't know the Lord. Somebody needs to witness to them who moves in their circles. It might as well be us. My husband reluctantly went along with it all, although he did not enjoy the social times with them and would just as soon have never been a part of any of it. He did it because he knew it meant so much to me.

"I would carefully watch to see what the next spending trend would be and follow it. It might be the year that 'they' were all taking a cruise, or the time 'they' were all redecorating, or putting in a sauna, or getting new stereo/video equipment, or getting a camper, etc. Whatever it was, it cost money we didn't have to buy stuff we didn't need, to keep up with people that I never felt comfortable with, and my husband didn't like!

"Yes, I felt convicted of my sin of overspending and not honoring my husband. But I felt driven to conform to 'their' standards. It was as though I was just being compelled. It was exhausting. There was always something new, something better that came along to do or to get. There was never any rest from the urgency of acquiring.

"Driving home from the cruise we couldn't afford, I was weary just thinking about how to pay for it all. We drove into the driveway. It was obvious something was very wrong. Where was the camper? With growing trepidation, all five of us got out of the car and headed slowly toward the front door, which was ajar. Looking inside, we gasped. The house had been completely ransacked. Everything of any value at all, including kitchen utensils, had been taken.

"There must have been a group of thieves working for hours loading up the camper, for the house to be so empty. Gone was all the stuff I felt I had to have to be like 'them.' Much of it was not even paid for yet.

"After the shock wore off, and the tears were shed, my husband said he knew it was the hand of the Lord getting our attention and stopping us from continuing in our foolishness. He said it would never happen again. Strangely, I felt a sense of relief. It had been so futile and so exhausting keeping up with 'them.' Well, 'they' really didn't care. Mostly, 'they' were just glad it had not happened to them.

"That was four years ago. We just made the last payment. The sense of freedom, of lightness, is impossible to describe. But what is an even greater feeling of joy is the sense of being in God's will, of choosing to please Him rather than 'them.' How odd! 'They' are such tough taskmasters. God is gracious, loving, merciful, and forgiving. My husband and I choose to obey the Lord!

"Years ago, my husband and I had selected Psalm 37:4–5 as our special verses: "Delight yourself also in the Lord, and He shall give you the desires of your heart. Commit your way to the Lord, trust also in Him, and He shall bring it to pass."

"Obviously we had strayed, and had allowed others to rule our desires, not the Lord. But we are back on track now, and stronger together and in the Lord than we have ever been. We thank God for getting our attention and bringing so much good out of it."

Sara

Sometimes the reality of financial catastrophe comes into a woman's life just like several earthquakes of increasing severity, shaking her to the core, and bringing life-changing aftershocks that last for years.

Sara is in her fifties, enthusiastic, gifted in many areas,

and glows with the light of the Lord. During the early years of her marriage, life was financially good and getting better. As she wisely says today, "A myth of my generation is that if you work hard and save, everything will be all right. That just isn't so." Sara graciously shares her story:

"When our children were entering their teens, we lived in the big house with all the goodies. Our home was the center of church and school activities. Both my husband and I wanted it that way. I was very involved with the children and their friends. That was my focus. The communication between my husband and me was not as good as it should have been, yet we always loved and respected each other. It simply took a backseat to the children during this time.

"When our last child was nearly through high school, I began to notice that my husband was depressed. Life didn't seem to be fun for him anymore. He was losing his sense of humor and becoming increasingly non-communicative. As he withdrew emotionally, I felt more and more isolated but didn't know what to do. 'I firmly believe that just as God can use doctors to heal broken bodies, so God can use counselors to heal broken hearts.' We sought out a Christian counselor.

"During the sessions, the subject of finances came up. I didn't have anything to do with the finances of the family. I trusted my husband completely and didn't think it was important for me to know what was going on. He gave me an allowance. I had certain responsibilities and bills to handle, which I did.

"All too soon, my life came crashing down. I didn't think there were any secrets, but I found out that my husband was deeply in debt. There were also problems with the IRS. We owed all this money. With interest and penalties it amounted to well over $300,000! I was stunned. I had just kept on spending like I always had. I assumed we were like other people, and had some debt, but nothing like this!

"I was so hurt and angry. I believed my husband didn't

trust me enough to tell me. I told him he should have told me. He told me he thought I knew. The financial downward spiral escalated. He lost his job. We lost the house and our investments. Security for me had been my home and family. Now we began to move continually. Each move was into something smaller, cheaper, less desirable.

"After several years of hanging on, we were in the process of going bankrupt. We lived on plastic in order to survive, because we didn't have enough money. As a result, some of the credit cards maxed out, and we were canceled even though I had paid mine in full each month.

"Several months ago it got so bad we could not pay the rent. Friends helped. Now I can understand *poor.* I never knew how to 'do' poor. Now I do. I don't buy anything. I don't go anywhere. I know what it is like to sit still and be quiet before the Lord.

"I don't eat out. I use a food co-op. I am very careful with electricity and water. I have learned to cook things I've never cooked before. My husband was a meat and potatoes guy. Now I keep a pot of soup going all the time, adding something to the pot each day. That means that I can still be hospitable. I am still able to share with others.

"I haven't bought an article of clothing in three years. I have a broken tooth, but I am not having dental work. I cut my hair and my husband's hair. Although I have loads of health problems, we don't have health insurance. But God is taking care of me in so many ways. I appreciate things so much now. I used to think that eating out was my right. Now, when friends take us out it is a special treat.

"Life is much simpler and easier now. Life is far less complicated than when I was getting and going and I had to have such and such. All that 'stuff' takes a lot of care. When earthquakes come, I have nothing to break. I don't have to hire someone to dust and vacuum a big place. I can do it all myself. And I like it.

"I would not choose to live where we are. I hate the thin walls and the noises of people talking and arguing. But God put us here, and I've never questioned it. I have no storage. I use cardboard boxes for a pantry.

"I've learned what sacrificial giving is. It is not giving from your extras. It is doing without completely so you can help someone else. I don't desire the things I used to. I don't think I ever will again. God has changed me. My focus is different, and it always will be. God has taught me some wonderful lessons that I couldn't have learned in any other way.

"I'm not telling you that I am not afraid when I don't know where rent and food money is coming from. But the big lesson is that although I am totally helpless, I am now confident that my great God is in control. I know He'll take care of my husband and me.

"I used to think that the Lord would bless me if I did all the right things. I found out that wasn't true. But I do know that my Lord is full of grace and mercy. If I told you that I feel privileged in a sense to go through what I've gone through, the women reading your book will think I'm nuts! But they haven't been there. God has made himself so very real to me during this time. I have experienced the truth of 2 Corinthians 12:9: 'My grace is sufficient for you, for My strength is made perfect in weakness. Therefore most gladly I will rather boast in my infirmities, that the power of Christ may rest upon me.' "

I asked Sara to explain her positive attitude. Immediately she referred to the book of Job. "I cling to Job 2:10, 13:15, and 19:25 and believe them with all my heart: 'Shall we indeed accept good from God and shall we not accept adversity?' . . . 'Though He slay me, yet will I trust Him.' . . . 'I know that my Redeemer lives.' "

Steps to God-Confidence in the Area of Possessions

Pour out the longings of your heart to God—*honestly!* That will always be the first step for each of us in building God-confidence. Of course, God already knows, but we need to be honest with Him and with ourselves in order to pinpoint exactly what the "self-esteem" destroyer is. When God has our attention in an honest, forthright way, He begins to build God-confidence in His child.

Do you know the difference between the wealthy and the rest of us? "They" have more things, of better quality, and do the expensive things more often!

First, let God know exactly what financial fears or what possessions are keeping you from attaining your coveted goal. Never be embarrassed or ashamed to do this with God. Expressing these desires to God is also a first step in getting a grip on His fiscal reality for you.

There is no hope for financial contentment until you first choose to be honest with God and with yourself.

Second, remember that our archenemy, Satan, wants us to be enslaved by the things of this world. This is a certain false hope, for contentment is always pursuing but never quite attaining, which convinces us that we would be content *if* we "just had such and such!" We know this is false, yet we get trapped—again and again and again!

If Satan can just keep our focus on stuff rather than on the Lord, he has us exactly where he wants us—in bondage! Our loving Lord wants us to be free in all areas, but freedom can only come by focusing on Him.

This little story may help to emphasize this point. The pastor's wife of a very small country church wanted to get a new dress for a special occasion. She knew she shouldn't spend the money, and she had three other dresses that would have served the purpose, but she went shopping. Sure enough, she found the dress that was the answer to her coveting for something new. Although the price was far too steep, she took it to the dressing room and tried it on. It looked great. The temptation was overwhelming! In an instant of hesitation, she cried, "Get thee behind me Satan." The response was immediate: "It looks great in the back, too!"

Satan will always be there to encourage us into fiscal bondage. He wants to destroy us and will use the "lust of the flesh, the lust of the eyes, and the pride of life" (1 John

2:16) to do it if given an opportunity.

Third, ask the Lord to make you content with what He's already given!

Being content with what I've got is a constant struggle for me, as well as for a lot of other Christian women. Just when I think I'm fairly content for the moment, I get an idea! And—you can be sure that the idea will cost money! It's absolutely uncanny! I don't know about you, but I can just walk through my home looking at things that could use replacing, refinishing, or refurbishing. If I followed through, it could cost thousands of dollars! Why don't I walk through my home praising the Lord for allowing me to have a lovely shelter, and for giving me so much? Because I am so deeply affected by this world's system.

Isn't it curious that just the feeling of desire and of wanting creates anxiety and stress? Well, we know that does not come from our gracious Lord! Richard Foster has also written a dynamic book entitled *Freedom of Simplicity*. In discussing the principle of contentment he writes:

> One of the most profound effects of inward simplicity is the rise of an amazing spirit of contentment. Gone is the need to strain and pull to get ahead. In rushes a glorious indifference to position, status, or possession. Living out of this wonderful Center causes all other concerns to fade into insignificance. So utterly immersed was St. Paul in this reality, that from a Roman prison he could write, "I have learned in whatever state I am, to be content" (Philippians 4:11). To be abased or to abound was a matter of indifference to him. Plenty and hunger, abundance and want were immaterial to this Jew with the Titan soul. "I can do all things through Christ who strengthens me," he said, and so he lived (Philippians 4:13).
>
> How cleverly Paul turned the tables on all those who taught that "godliness is a means of gain" by replying that "godliness with contentment is great gain" (1 Timothy 6:5–6). He saw that the problem with material gain is its inability to bring contentment. John

D. Rockefeller was once asked how much money it would take to be really satisfied. He answered, "Just a little bit more!" And that is precisely our problem—it always takes a little more; contentment remains elusive.

But the wonderful thing about simplicity is its ability to give us contentment. Do you understand what a freedom this is? To live in contentment means we can opt out of the status race and the maddening pace that is its necessary partner. We can shout, "No!" to the insanity that chants, "More, more, more!" We can rest contented in the gracious provision of God.[2]

Perhaps one of the most apparent positive results of the Northridge earthquake is that those who have suffered enormous loss of material possessions have learned how little any of it means. When confronted with the mercy of God in allowing the lives of loved ones to be preserved, cleaning up piles of debris resulting from our lifelong love affair with the accumulation of possessions seemed like just a routine chore.

Not one woman I know, including myself, has any desire to replace all the "stuff" that was broken, shattered, or marred as a result of the quake. We are thankful for what God allowed to remain, and will be very careful when using the money that God has provided to purchase "stuff" that can be utterly destroyed in seconds. You can safely assume that our value system took a-shaking and a-quaking, and, thankfully, will never be the same again.

Fourth: "But seek first the kingdom of God and His righteousness, and all these things shall be added to you" (Matthew 6:33).

Have you ever heard of George Mueller? He was a man with great passions and struggles with money who lived in the 1800s. He is a shining example of the God-confidence that can be built in a life yielded to the Lord.

He was his father's favorite and was given money freely. Instead of learning how to use it and save it, he learned careless waste and indulgence. Worse than that, when his father asked for an account of the money given, he would lie and deceive to cover his spending habits. "Whenever his tricks were discovered he would devise more ingenious devices of trickery and fraud.

"Before he was ten years old he was a habitual thief and an expert at cheating. . . . The night his mother lay dying, her boy of fourteen was reeling through the streets, drunk. Even her death failed to arrest his wicked course.

"At sixteen, he was drawn by his passion for a girl to spend time in costly hotels. He ran up bills until, payment being demanded, he had to leave his best clothes as security, barely escaping arrest. When he tried the bold scheme in another town, he was caught and sent to jail.

"Dissipation continued to drag him into the mire of debt. When his allowance could not help him out, he resorted to the most ingenious devices of falsehood. Once he pretended that his money had been stolen by violence. Forcing the locks of his trunk and guitar case, he ran to his friends half dressed, feigning fright, declaring that he was the victim of a robbery. He excited such pity that his friends made up a purse to cover his supposed losses.

"After twenty years of evil-doing, George Mueller was converted to God, and the radical nature of the change in him strikingly proves and displays the sovereignty of Almighty Grace."[3]

The Lord used George Mueller to build five large orphan houses in England that took care of over 10,000 orphans. George Mueller also gave aid to day-schools and Sunday schools in England, where nearly 150,000 children were taught. He circulated nearly two million Bibles and over three million books and tracts. Besides all this, he aided missionaries in various lands. The sum total of the money spent during his 60 years in service to the Lord totaled over $7.5 million! This figure is particularly astonishing when we consider what $1.00 could purchase between 1825 and 1885.

How did a man who never had enough money for pleasure have the capacity to obtain millions for God? He learned to do God's will in God's way, and the Lord gave the increase.

As a believer, his philosophy toward obtaining money for his orphanages and other works is particularly fascinating. "It is not enough to obtain means for the work of God, but that these means should be obtained in God's way. To ask unbelievers for means is not God's way; to press even believers to give is not God's way."[4] (Now isn't that revolutionary?)

George Mueller made a pact with the Lord never to ask anyone for money directly, nor even state the needs in such a way as to indirectly appeal for aid. He believed these methods to be "forms of trusting in the arm of the flesh, instead of going at once, always, and only, to the Lord."

"He stated that at various times, not only at the beginning of the work, but also in later years, God had seen fit to try his faith to the utmost, but only to prove to him the more definitely that He would never be other than his faithful covenant-keeping God. In illustration, he referred to a time when, the children having had their last meal for the day, there was nothing left in money or kind for their breakfast the following morning. Mr. Mueller went home, but nothing came in, and he retired for the night, committing the need to God to provide. Early the next morning he went for a walk, and while praying for the needed help he took a turn into a road that he was quite unconscious of, and after walking a short distance, a friend met him and said how glad he was to meet him and asked him to accept five pounds for the orphans. Mr. Mueller thanked him and without saying a word to the donor about the time of need, he went at once to the orphan houses, praising God for this direct answer to prayer."[5]

To George Mueller, God was *Jehovah-Jireh*—The-Lord-Will-Provide (Genesis 22:14). That same heavenly Father will provide for you and for me. As we trust and obey, we can have the God-confidence to know that He "is able to do exceedingly abundantly above all that we ask or think" (Ephesians 3:20).

Fifth, get serious in prayer with the Lord about freedom from debt and from wanting "stuff"!

George Mueller referred to prayer as his great secret. "Such a life and such a work are the result of one habit more than all else—daily and frequent communion with God. Unwearied in supplications and intercessions, in every new need and crisis, prayer was the one resort, the prayer of faith. He was an unwearied intercessor. No delay discouraged him."

That's the way it's got to be with you and me. When I really, really want something, I am attempting to go directly to my *Jehovah-Jireh* and discuss it with Him. I ask the Lord to either give me whatever it is, or to take away the desire and keep me from the folly of foolish spending! Because God wants to lead us into financial solvency and fiscal responsibility, He answers any honest plea. It is amazing how my flaming desire is extinguished through prayer. Other times, the Lord allows me to wait and provides the financial means over time.

God works in different ways to accomplish His purposes for you and me. Naturally, He would. After all, He's the God of infinite creativity and variety and diversity. Just look around you!

One thing is very certain: He hears and answers earnest prayer . . . always! Of course often the answer is *no*. Many times the answer is *wait*. Sometimes it is *yes*! Our God, noted for compassion and lovingkindness, answers each prayer in accordance with what is best for us as He—the all-knowing and all-powerful God of the universe—sees it. That really should be enough for you and me.

Sixth, rejoice and give thanks to God for what He is teaching you in this crucial area of life.

Don't be discouraged, and don't give up! At times, I make progress and then slip back into my old spending habits. The Lord corrects, forgives, encourages, and I make a little more progress. That's a life pattern for most of us in all areas, including finances and the lust for stuff. God does correct our attitudes and actions. Isn't that enough encouragement to increase God-confidence?

Seventh, M&M—*Memorize and Meditate.*

Are you beginning to discover that memorizing God's Word and thinking about it during the day builds God-confidence quicker than anything? Such is the cleansing and healing power of the Word of God!

Let's review the verses from this chapter:

Pat: Isaiah 55:8–9—" 'For My thoughts are not your thoughts, nor are your ways My ways,' says the Lord. 'For as the heavens are higher than the earth, so are My ways higher than your ways, and My thoughts than your thoughts.' "

2 Corinthians 10:4–5—"For the weapons of our warfare are not carnal but mighty in God for pulling down strongholds, casting down arguments and every high thing that exalteth itself against the knowledge of God, bringing every thought into captivity to the obedience of Christ."

Lamentations 3:21–24—"This I recall to my mind, therefore I have hope. Through the Lord's mercies we are not consumed, because His compassions fail not. They are new every morning; great is Your faithfulness. 'The Lord is my portion,' says my soul, 'therefore I hope in Him!' "

Beverly: Psalm 37:4–5—"Delight yourself also in the Lord, and He shall give you the desires of your heart. Commit your way to the Lord, trust also in Him, and He shall bring it to pass."

Sara: 2 Corinthians 12:9—"My grace is sufficient for you, for my strength is made perfect in weakness."

Job 2:10b—"Shall we indeed accept good from God, and shall we not accept adversity?"

Job 13:15—"Though He slay me, yet will I trust Him."

Job 19:25—"For I know that my Redeemer lives."

Paul: Philippians 4:11—"I have learned in whatever state I am, to be content."

Philippians 4:13—"I can do all things through Christ who strengthens me."

1 Timothy 6:6—"But godliness with contentment is great gain."

George Mueller: Matthew 6:33—"But seek first the kingdom of God and His righteousness, and all these things shall be added to you."

Genesis 22:14—"The Lord Will Provide."

Hebrews 13:8—"Jesus Christ is the same yesterday, today, and forever."

Ephesians 3:20—"Now to Him who is able to do exceedingly abundantly above all that we ask or think, according to the power that works in us, to Him be glory in the church by Christ Jesus throughout all ages, world without end. Amen."

Reflections

1. Write a "Money Autobiography." Consider the place of money in your childhood. What view of money did your parents have? Did you feel deprived or privileged? How are those influences affecting you today?

_____

_____

_____

_____

2. What are your two biggest frustrations in life when it comes to having and getting of "things"? Be specific.

_____

_____

_____

_____

3. Are you a compulsive shopper and spender? Why or why not?

_____

_____

_____

_____

4. Do you buy things to impress people? To "feel better"? Or does spending money mostly make you feel anxious? Please explain.

_____

_____

_____

_____

_____

_____

5. How do the shopping habits and purchases of other people influence your spending?

_____

_____

_____

_____

_____

6. G. K. Chesterton once said, "There are two ways to get enough: one is to continue to accumulate more and more. The other is to desire less." Please comment on how this could apply to you.

_____

_____

_____

_____

_____

_____

7. Carefully review each of the seven steps to God-confidence in the area of possessions, and write a personal comment on each one.

_____

_____

_____

_____

_____

_____

8. Select one or more verses for your own personal "M&M." Write them down.

_____

_____

_____

_____

_____

_____

_____

9. After you have committed the first verse to memory, and are beginning to think about it during the day, explain how God is using it in your life.

_____

_____

_____

_____

_____

_____

Date of response_____

Myth Seven

Oh, Lord, I know you are a sovereign God—working all things into your plan. As you know, I feel overwhelmed and out of control. I'm overworked, overcommitted, over-peopled, overscheduled, overextended, overburdened, over-tired, overwrought—over and over and over again.

Life has become a race against time, and I'm getting far-ther and farther behind. Oh, dear God, something is ter-ribly wrong. I know this is not what you want for me! Please, please help me get control of my time and my life before I self-destruct from the pressures!

"With All I Have to Do, I Can Never Feel Finished."

THE "LIFESTYLE OF THE IRRITABLE AND exhausted is far removed from the simple life most of us would like to live.

Do you ever wake up annoyed with all that's ahead in your day? Do you sometimes go through the day in neutral, never quite getting into gear?

Just contemplating the commitments and responsibilities of the day ahead fatigues me sometimes. What really moves me from minor irritability into major league anger is realizing how much of what I have to do I have brought on myself. How? By opening my very *big* mouth and saying that killer word—*yes*. Then I not only lack confidence in my ability to "beat the clock," something in me feels weak and violated—when I'm the one who has invaded my own life and given it away to other people, other purposes!

As the stack of commitments surrounding my day becomes deeper, I consider one of three possible ways the little word *yes* has been a big killjoy to confidence and contentment:

1. Someone, somewhere, suggested something to do at sometime, and in a moment of emotional exuberance, I stupidly said, "I'd love to." *I'd been included. How nice!* Others I knew had not been invited. I was feeling good. I was certain I'd have time and could work it out.

2. Someone called. I was too rushed to talk and suggested, "Let's get together." As we were setting the future date I felt safe and secure. With my current schedule, I wasn't even certain I'd be alive by then! So there would be

no problem in keeping the commitment.

3. Someone, somewhere, talked about something that needed to be done. *No one* had volunteered to do it. The person knew I could do it. At that point it didn't matter to me whether I could or should. I didn't want to say *no* and feel guilty. So I said *yes*—and am now on the verge of a raging tantrum. My poor family! They will be the ones to suffer for my guilty *yes*. That was then and this is now. I'm older now than when I foolishly said *yes* in my guilt-ridden zeal of two weeks ago.

Searching my foggy brain for a way out of my self-inflicted mess, I swallow. I am certain a sore throat is threatening. Since I am almost always on the brink of bronchitis, questionable health is a possible excuse. Then the argument begins. "You don't want to be seen by others as undependable, do you? You know how they talk when somebody lets them down at the last minute. You know how you talk when someone is suspected of manufacturing a lame excuse! Besides, you know that being a responsible Christian woman is honoring to the Lord. You said you would be there and do it. Others are counting on you. Are you going to let them down? Someone's feelings will be hurt. How can they get a replacement at this late date? Do you want to live in guilt for the rest of your life? *Maybe you'll really get sick if you use illness as an excuse!*" (This is when other superstitious thinking kicks in!)

While these happy thoughts are hurling in my head, I get ready, grumbling as I go: Sometimes my bad attitude disgusts even me! First I blame "them." Then I blame me. Why do I insist on living a people-pressured life? Why am I doing this to myself? When will I ever learn? I've been running on empty for too long, trying to do too much in too little time. . . .

By now, I'm stalking through the house, and what catches my pantherlike gaze? Mountains of laundry, layers of dust, and hills of bills. Me? I've plunged to the bottom of the valley of despair. And this is before the day "officially" begins!

One thing is absolutely certain. Unless something changes drastically, I am guaranteed to have a "Terrible, Horrible, No Good, Very Bad Day."[1]

Management by Insanity

Variations of this sad little saga are repeated at some time by every honest Christian woman I know. Regardless of age or stage of life, Christian women have trouble with managing their time. The crush of time itself is a major destroyer of confidence. One frustrated friend said, "Time Management? You must be crazy! I don't need that. I have no time of my own to manage. Everybody's got a piece, and there is not one single minute left for me!"

Another friend quipped, "If it weren't for the last minute, I'd never get anything done!"

A third told me, "I feel like a baseball player. The day delivers the hard, fast pitch. It curves into my life. I bunt and begin the dash from place to place. Out of breath, I skid from this to that. At the end of the day, nearly falling down, I slide into home."

A well-respected Christian leader, a woman who is very involved in numerous worthwhile activities, confided, "I am on a nonstop treadmill of hyperactive 'Churchianity.' Sometimes, I'm literally breathless from the continuous effort of doing and going. The women who said they'd help all disappear when the going gets tough, and I'm left to do it all. Honestly, if breathing took any time out of my day it would have to be eliminated. I'm always going somewhere to do something for somebody else. Hey! What about me? I'm a wreck! I know I shouldn't say this, but sometimes I just want to run away. I feel like writing a note, 'I love you. Goodbye.' I need my space. When is it ever going to be my turn?"

Women of all walks of life feel the pressure of time. My daughter was serving on a summer missions trip in the inner-city of Brooklyn, New York. She was getting ready to serve in a soup kitchen. "The line was forming," Candice remembers. "A lady in the front had been waiting for no longer than five minutes. She had a very disgusted look on her face. The lady put her hands on her hips, looked around, glaring, and with great disdain announced, 'I have PMS! I don't have time to be waiting around like this!' " Just imagine! A woman in line for a handout didn't have five minutes to wait for a free lunch!

In my times of super stress, I fantasize about having one day in the week that nobody knows about. A day where I can just get caught up, organized, and rested without intervention or interruption from anybody! But since that will never be for you or for me, what are we to do?

The good news is that there are answers. The Lord is ready, willing, and able to get our lives and times under control. The tougher news is that we must *choose* to implement His will for us. God is not going to force us into organizing our time according to His will—although many times I wish He would forcibly stop me midsentence! He has given us power of choice. Naturally, there are always consequences. As we have seen, outside of the Lord's direction, these actions can create a "load limit" of self-induced stress. God would never put on us what we allow other people to load us down with or what we load on ourselves.

Leading people-pressured lives is very much like being a puppet on a string. "They" pull our strings, and we respond, just like brainless puppets. It might be the string of pride, guilt, envy, of needing to be needed or accepted, or one of a host of other strings. Yes, "they" know the right moves to get us to move in the direction they wish.

And probably the things they're pressuring us to do are good things. So what! If we're doing anything because of pressure from other people rather than because of God's leading, those things are wrong for us!

A God-confident woman knows how to graciously say *no*. For me, having the confidence to say *no* freed me from the slavery of overinvolvement. So how do I know when to say *yes* and when to say *no*? By discussing every single thing with my Father, the Creator of time, and the only One who can give solid guidance and direction. Every one of us can grow in God-confidence that helps us to say, "Thank you for asking, but I'm not certain. Let me pray about it first." Or, "I'll get back to you."

Living the Present in His Presence

There are other times when you and I will have the clear leading of the Holy Spirit to respond with a firm *yes!* or *no!* on the spot. Of course, in order to be sensitive to the leading of the Holy Spirit, we must cultivate a habit of continual communication with the Lord.

Ideally, praying is like breathing. Prayer needs to flow through our day like oxygen through our body. Wouldn't it be ridiculous to try to take a gulp of oxygen in the morning that was large enough to get through the day? It is equally preposterous to think that all the praying that is necessary can be done during an early morning quiet time. You and I can literally "practice the presence of Christ" through prayer all day long.

"But you don't understand," you may be thinking. "I don't have five seconds to call my own from the time I get up until I pass out on the pillow at night. I know I should pray, but it's not reality for me right now!"

First of all, almost no one that I know has "time" to pray. People who pray take the time. People who pray make the time. Why? Because they realize that praying is to the spiritual life what breathing is to the physical body. Most of us are weighed down with spiritual emergency oxygen tanks because we will not pray until a crisis or an emergency makes panic prayer crucial.

I've tried it both ways—prayer as breathing, and prayer as panic. I can promise you, on my word as a Christian, that for every second you spend in prayer, the Lord multiplies the time in your day. And He does it by giving you calmness and focus, giving wisdom in making decisions. Our awesome God will even begin to develop in you a quality that many of us long for—*serenity!*

Susanna Wesley knew a great deal about leading a busy life. She married at nineteen. Two years later, she gave birth to her first child. Within the next twenty-one years, she gave birth to eighteen other children. She undertook the education of the children and oversaw the house and fields. In addition to her rigorous home duties, she wrote three religious textbooks for children. Her home became a center of encouragement and spiritual ministry in the community. And all this flowed out of a life of prayer.

"Her steadfast prayer life was her outstanding characteristic. No matter what might intervene, when the clock struck certain hours, she retired to her room for prayer.

"One legend concerning this remarkable woman tells that when the children got exasperating, Susannah would toss the hem of her long white apron over her head to hide her face for prayer. When they saw Mother with her apron up, the children walked softly."[2]

Susanna's son John Wesley wrote of her: "For many years my mother was employed in abundance of temporal business. Yet she never suffered anything to break in upon her time for prayer and meditation, which she sacredly observed."[3]

Life Has a Certain "Ring" to It

Frankly, I used to wonder, *How would this biography read if Susanna had a telephone?* What do you think?

I've thought a lot about this through the years as I have fumed in frustration as too much time has slipped by, gone forever, while I gabbed on the phone.

I like to be charitable and believe that Susanna Wesley would not have been trapped by the tyranny of the telephone. She would have been the master of this wonderful communication vehicle, not its slave.

Not wanting to have my children think that they were less important than whoever was on the other end of the insistent ring, they knew that at certain times Mommy was not going to answer the phone. For example, in our home the phone had no priority over Family Devotions, Bible Story and Prayer Times, Family Talks, Family Game Times, Family Dinners, Individual Devotional Times, Nap Times, and most times when we had guests.

It is interesting to note that when the telephone first came into use in this country, it was only the privileged who had them in their homes. People of vast wealth, such as the Vanderbilts, used the phone as an intercommunication within their palatial residences. Since it was considered "rude" to intrude on the privacy of a neighbor via telephone, common communications were taken by servants on foot to the doors of the neighbors and given to other servants.

Those were the days! Privacy in the home was considered something normal to pursue and preserve. The omnipresent answering machine is today's answer to the pursuit of privacy in our homes!

I must confess, I delight in privacy and am somewhat passionate about preserving it in my home. Very often, when circumstances permit, I will turn the telephone off, or take it off the hook. Seems rather shocking, doesn't it? But don't knock it until you've tried it. A mini-vacation from outside voices is really quite a treat and enables you to fully concentrate on the needs of your family, your own needs, and do the myriad of things in your home that scream, "When are you going to get to me?"

But, you may say, "People have problems. They need to talk. I can't ignore those needs, can I?" Yes, people have needs, enormous needs—always! No matter how young or old you are, you have family and friends that are screaming out for someone to listen, to understand.

This is just one more instance of our needing the Lord's unfathomable wisdom and discernment, which is available to each of us, His children. People with problems want to talk, and they seek out people who are sensitive and understanding listeners (like you!). Invariably, they need your ear the most when you have the least time. This is where the wisdom and discernment of the Lord is crucial—to them, and to the preservation of your own sanity.

Let's say that someone you love dearly has just called. You answer, although you are on the way out the door to do something special with the family. Your friend's life is "falling apart." She is weeping uncontrollably. You can hardly make out the words. This is a terrible dilemma, and one that probably happens more frequently than we care to mention.

Pastor Eric, a dear man who does justly, loves mercy, and walks humbly with His God (Micah 6:8), gave me the best answer to use at such times. With great joy, I share it with you. "I can't give you the time you deserve right now." Isn't that the brilliance of the Lord? The comment is gracious, kind, respectful, understanding, and compassionate of the person's needs, yet does not pull you away from the priority of the moment. You then have the opportunity of arranging a convenient time to speak with the person. This also enables you to enter the future conversation prayerfully prepared. Letting the person know you will be keeping them in your prayers "between now and then" is a Godsend to anyone who understands that the "effective, fervent prayer of a righteous man [or woman] avails much" (James 5:16). Very often I have found that by the time I contact the person at the appointed time, God has already been at work. (Big surprise.) That hurting person needed my prayers more than any human words. Seeing God at work in answered prayer is a major way of developing God-confidence.

I have to add this little comment. It's too bad that needy people like you and me don't choose to spend more time talking with the only One who can soothe our sorrows. Think of the difference it would make if each of us would spend as much time talking with the Lord as we spend talking with everyone else, if we would pick up the Word before we pick up the phone!

I find that very convicting. It is easier for each of us to spend more time moaning and groaning with other people than to talk to the Almighty Solver of Every Problem. In my Bible, I have written this penetrating question: "Why pray when you can worry?" I have to smile. Far, far too often I worry aloud rather than praying silently. How foolish! I know better, and yet I fail again and again. But each time, the Lord of the second, third, fourth chances is there to forgive, to encourage, and to give another opportunity!

Steps to God-Confidence in the Area of Time Management

First, take the time to pray through your schedule frustrations. Our gracious Lord does not weary of hearing our woes. "His ear [is not] so dull that it cannot hear" (Isaiah 59:1, NASB). The Lord "knows our frame; He is mindful that we are but dust" (Psalm 103:14, NASB). He has great and abiding compassion for the sheep of His pasture. Always remember that sheep are not burden-bearing animals. They are not designed for this purpose. Whenever you or I attempt to bear burdens that our Good Shepherd needs to carry, we become weighed down, oppressed, and can never be joyful or successful.

Equipped with a shepherd's experience and insight, Phillip Keller relates, "It is no accident that God has chosen to call us sheep. Sheep do not 'just take care of themselves' as some might suppose. They require, more than any other class of livestock, endless attention and meticulous care.

"The behavior of sheep and human beings is similar in many ways. Our mass mind (or mob instincts), our fear and timidity, our stubbornness and stupidity, and our perverse habits are all parallels of profound importance.

"Yet despite these adverse characteristics, Christ chooses us, buys us, calls us by name, makes us His own and delights in caring for us."[4] What better encouragement could we sheep have for being completely honest and forthright with our Good Shepherd?

Second, cultivate the habit of beginning each day by focusing on the Lord.

When you are in the first stages of groggy consciousness, that's the time to think about the Lord and give your day to Him. No matter how I feel, or what I have to do, or what I am afraid might or might not happen, I strive to say, "This is the day which the Lord has made; let us rejoice and be glad in it" (Psalm 118:24, NASB). Just saying this verse encourages me and helps to set an attitude attack for the day. It is very important to me to pray this and other verses before getting out of bed. After all, a lot can happen between lifting your head from the pillow and putting your feet on the floor! It is a matter of choosing your attitude before you begin your day—either a tyrannized mindset, or a mind and heart focused on God.

Perhaps you've heard the little ditty, "Each day is a gift. That's why it's called *the present.*" That is a good reminder for Christian women. My problem is that too often I want to return the gift, unopened, and exchange it for something else! I should approach the day like this: This is the beginning of a new day. God has given me this day to use as I will. I can waste it or use it for good. What I do today is important, because I'm exchanging a day of my life for it. When tomorrow comes, this day will be gone forever, leaving something I have traded for it. I want it to be gain, not loss; good, not evil; success, not failure; in order that I shall not regret the price I paid for it.

A Prayer for My Time

Years ago, I wrote a time management prayer I'd like to share with you:

Dear Heavenly Father,
    Thank you for your loving care and protection throughout the night. I give to you this day—every moment and hour in it, and thank you for it.
    Please guide my ways, and show me how to use my

time effectively and efficiently. There is so much to do. Please help me to get it done and to do it well, with love, joy, and thanksgiving. Teach me to do your will.

Give me the wisdom to know when to say *yes* and the courage to say *no* to the things that detract from your will for my life.

Use me this day. Take my thoughts, attitudes, actions, and words and make them pleasing to you. May all I do, say, and think bring honor and glory to your holy Name.

Third, realize that God never asks, expects, or wants us to "do it all!"

It is completely unnecessary pressure we put on ourselves when we attempt to please and placate people—which is an impossible task, anyway! Attempting to win the praise, admiration, and respect of people while going crazy in the maze we've created out of life will lead to disappointment and failure. Leading a people-pressured life means that we have put people and their judgments ahead of God's direction. It is a form of idolatry and will never give us confidence, peace, joy, or contentment.

Phyllis needed to return to teaching to finance private Christian education for her children. She and her husband had sought the Lord's wisdom and believed this was His will for them.

Her children attended the school where she was beginning to teach. "I enjoyed going to school each day with my children, and they enjoyed having me there. I was already committed to the choir at church, the social committee for Sunday school, and was always available for church responsibilities where I was needed. That was just my lifestyle. It was a lot of work, but I like doing everything. My husband was a tremendous help at home. We worked as a team. He was very supportive and encouraging. It was a nice arrangement, and I thought all was going well.

"It was the Easter season. My church always put on a spectacular production, which required many evening practices and some Saturdays. On this particular evening,

I fed the family while my husband supervised the baths and did the dishes. I graded papers. Before I rushed off to choir practice, I went to say good-night to my five-year-old Debra. After we kissed and hugged, she looked up at me with a very serious expression and said, 'Mommies don't have time for little girls anymore.'

"I felt like I'd been stabbed. I left her room and cried my heart out. I had heard truth from the mouth of a child. That night I talked to the Lord and my husband. He also felt I was too fragmented in my activities. The Easter production was my last choir activity. I learned to save grading until after bedtime. The Lord used my daughter to get my attention and remind me that my children needed to be my priority over all the other 'stuff.' I am thankful that He did this early in the child-raising years."

When my children were tiny, I attended a Bible study led by a woman named Allegra Harrah. Because she was the mother of eight children, I thought I'd better listen carefully to anything she had to say. Other women agreed. Over 300 women from various churches gathered on Wednesday mornings to hear her teach. One day, several women were voicing requests for prayer. Each had to do with frenetic schedules. They couldn't cope. It was all too much. When they were through, she looked over the audience of eager faces with a sober face, paused for a long moment, and then said, "Girls, you can simplify your lives." She stopped to let this sink in, then repeated with emphasis, "You really can simplify your lives."

I have never forgotten those words. They are as true today, for you and me, as they were then. If you call upon the Lord He will answer and will show you just exactly how you can simplify your life to conform to what is His best for you. I love this little saying, "God knows. God loves. God cares. Nothing this truth can dim. God gives the very best to those who leave the choice to Him."

Fourth, meditate on the fact that Jesus, our ultimate role model, never rushed around . . . and He only had three years of ministry to get the job done. Even so, He got away from people often to spend time alone in blissful solitude with His heavenly Father.

"He inaugurated His ministry by spending forty days alone in the desert (Matthew 4:1–11). Before He chose the twelve He spent the entire night alone in the desert hills (Luke 6:12). When He received the news of the death of John the Baptist, 'He withdrew from there in a boat, to a lonely place by Himself' (Matthew 14:13, NASB). After the miraculous feeding of the five thousand, Jesus made His disciples leave; 'and after he had dismissed the crowds, he went up into the hills by himself to pray' (Matthew 14:23, RSV). Following a long night of work, 'in the morning, having risen a long while before daylight, he went out and departed to a solitary place . . .' (Mark 1:35). When the twelve had returned from a preaching and healing mission, Jesus instructed them, 'Come aside by yourselves to a deserted place and rest a while' (Mark 6:31). Following the healing of a leper Jesus 'withdrew into the wilderness and prayed' (Luke 5:16). With three disciples He sought out the silence of a lonely mountain as the stage for the transfiguration (Matthew 17:1–9). As He prepared for His highest and most holy work, Jesus sought the solitude of the Garden of Gethsemane (Matthew 26:36–46). One could go on, but perhaps this is sufficient to show that the seeking out of a solitary place was a regular practice with Jesus. So it should be for us."[5]

Seeking solitude involves sacrifice. I can guarantee it. Some women get up early to experience the joy of solitude. Others stay up late. For the past several years, I have been waking up somewhere between 2:00 and 4:00 A.M. on a regular basis. This used to annoy me more than I can possibly communicate. I treasure a good night's sleep, and have been convinced that I must have at least eight hours in order to function with a modicum of alertness. One day, I was groaning about my sleep deprivation. My main prayer partner at school, Trudi, listened quietly, then said, "Maybe the Lord wants you awake to pray." That insightful comment turned on the light of understanding and acceptance for me. No longer do I bitterly complain about "not sleeping." Now I use those wakeful hours to pray and to worship in the hushed silence. I can talk with God about things, and in the peaceful cloak of night I'm prepared to listen. It is also a great time to quote Scripture and to meditate. Then, in due time, I fall into a peaceful, unburdened sleep.

Fifth, ask the Lord to give you the wisdom to know when to say *yes* and the courage to say *no*.

This begins, of course, by centering your life in a few prayerfully chosen areas of focus. After that, carefully evaluate each "opportunity." You do not need to be the first to say *yes*. In fact, you never need to say *yes* if it's outside an area of focus that's clearly not for you.

Richard Foster captures our frantic rush of daily life in his challenging book *The Freedom of Simplicity:*

> We dash here and there desperately trying to fulfill the many obligations that press in upon us. We jerk back and forth between business commitments and family responsibilities. While we are busy responding to the needs of child or spouse, we feel guilty about neglecting the demands of work. When we respond to the pressures of work, we fear we are failing our family. In those rare times when we are able to juggle the two successfully, the wider issues of nation and world whisper pestering calls to service. If anyone needs a simplification of life, we do.[6]

I don't know how to break this to you, but . . . the success of your church, your job, or your pet ministry does not rest on you. Your responsibility and mine is to do the Father's will in His way and leave the results to Him. The work of the church of Jesus Christ has been going on for generations before you, and if the Lord tarries, it will go on long after you.

Jesus Christ himself did not do it all. He did not heal everybody, feed everybody, or speak to everybody. He certainly did not *please* everybody! He had perfect God-confidence. In His own words, He came to "do the will of Him who sent Me" (John 4:34), and He did it.

You and I can take plenty of time to pray before making a decision to serve. You and I can take the time to count the cost, to seek the wisdom of our family and those who know and love us. Then, when the decision is made, we will feel confident that if we said *yes*, He will give us the time and energy and other resources to do the job "heartily, as to the Lord" (Colossians 3:23). If you or I say *no* we will be confident enough to realize that God has someone else in mind to do the work, and we will be able to accept the fact that they might even do a better job than we could have done. But if they don't, that's OK too, because God did not call us to do the job.

One way I force myself to take the time to make prayerful decisions is by *not* carrying around a calendar with me everywhere I go. Now I know that many women like to do so because it works for them. When asked to do something or go somewhere, they pull open the calendar to check, and give an immediate answer. I prefer to go a little slower to avoid overcommitment. I know that it is all too easy for me to say *yes* on the spur of the moment and then live with the regretful decision. I write down the date, check it against other dates and responsibilities, pray about the matter, then give the answer. It helps me. Perhaps it will be of use to you also.

Sixth, ask God to give you the wisdom to know how to organize and manage efficiently and effectively the time He has given to you. After all, He created time, so it is in His power to train us to use it the best possible way to accomplish what He desires.

The crucial time management question is, "What is the best use of my time right now?"

That is always an appropriate question to ask during the day. Sometimes the answer is to get alone and pray. Sometimes it's as simple as "Do the dishes!" or "Get off the phone!" Other times the answer may be "Take a nap." Ask the Lord, believing that He really cares and that He really will answer in a specific way that will strengthen your God-confidence.

At the age of thirty-four, Dwight L. Moody found out the good can be the enemy of the best!

The Chicago Fire of 1871 left him physically exhausted, mentally confused, emotional undone, and spiritually dry. "Whichever way he looked, the city lay in ashes. Gone were his elegant new home, his church and mission Sunday school, handsome Farwell Hall—less than a year old and built at great personal cost to him.

" 'One thousand children and their parents are looking to me for another building,' he wrote. For years now, Chicago had been looking to D. L. Moody. His life was an endless string of committee meetings, fund-raisers, conventions, and pastoral duties.

"It wasn't just the fire that had him down. He had been at low ebb for months. Now he began to cry out to God as never before, begging the Lord to fill him with His Holy Spirit.

"Sometime later, alone with God, Moody realized that it was not what he could do for God, but what God could do for him that mattered most. 'God revealed himself to me, and I had such an experience of His love that I had to ask Him to stay His hand,' Moody said when questioned about his transformation. 'I went to preaching again. The sermons were not different; I did not present any new truths, and yet hundreds were converted. I would not now be placed back where I was before that blessed experience if you should give me all the world—it would be as the small dust of the balance.'

"Soon, Moody sailed for England as a traveling evangelist, leaving the fund-raising and rebuilding to others. He lost interest in everything except preaching the Word and working for souls. As never before, Moody knew who Christ was, who he was, and what his purpose in life must be. His rebirth of confidence made him equal to the demands of international evangelism.

"A Spirit-transformed Moody was able to say, 'When

God wants to move a mountain, He does not take a bar of iron, but He takes a little worm. The fact is, we have too much strength. We are not weak enough. It is not our strength that we want. One drop of God's strength is worth more than all the world.' "[7]

Seventh, learn to "wait on the Lord!"

That is hard. Especially in an age where, if the microwave takes longer than thirty seconds, we complain, "This thing is taking forever!" Truly, we are living in an age of instant gratification. Whether it is food, clothing, shelter, communication, or a plethora of extras, we want what we want, and we want it now!

How curious that the Lord has not changed to keep up with our frenzy. The Lord does not always choose to give us His answers with the snap of a finger, the click of a switch, or the press of a button. He can, and sometimes does, but more often He requires us to pray and wait for His answer. Ever wonder why? Because God is more interested in teaching us about His ways and himself, and in building our character, than in capitulating to our fleshly nature!

Jeanne, an attractive, enthusiastic young mother, had known the Lord for only two years. Yet, in that time, the Lord had shown her much of who He was and how He worked. Another lesson was on the way.

She had applied for admission to our school late in February. "My heart's desire was to have my children attend a Christian school," Jeanne says with strength. "I did not have that opportunity." She was interested in enrollment for the following September when her oldest would be ready for first grade. The classes were full. Our registrar assured her that a lot can happen in a few months, and not only that, she was first on the waiting list. Jeanne relates: "I was not too concerned. Time went by. In June, there were still no openings. Friends began to ask, 'What are you going to do?' I went to my Father, and each time was assured that this school was the one for my family.

"Every few weeks, I called the school. Still no openings.

Brochures from other schools came in the mail. I wondered if this was a sign from the Lord. Should I visit other schools and check them out? I prayed. The answer seemed clear. *Trust Me.*

"My husband and I were likeminded. We both felt the Lord was clearly directing us to continue to wait on Him.

"By the end of the summer, there were still no openings. I began to ask the Lord, 'Am I being irresponsible?' The answer seemed to be the same. *Trust Me.*

"I clung to the truths of Proverbs 3:5–6: 'Trust in the Lord with all your heart, and lean not on your own understanding; in all your ways acknowledge Him, and He shall direct your paths.' And so I waited, believing that the Lord means what He says, believing that He is worthy of trust.

"The day before school was to open, I called. *Still no openings.* I called out to the Lord, 'You know how much I desire my son to be able to be there the first day.' There was no glimmer of hope. I comforted myself with Isaiah 40:31: 'But those who wait on the Lord shall renew their strength; they shall mount up with wings like eagles, they shall run and not be weary, they shall walk and not faint.'

"The next day school began—without my son. I was feeling pretty low. I took the children to the park. Even the sand was a problem. There were ants crawling all through it. I was really hurting.

"I asked the Lord for a word of encouragement. At the Bible bookstore, I bought my children each a Scripture cookie. The lady asked if I would like one. At first I replied, 'No, thank you!' then said, 'Okay,' thinking God might use the verse to bring encouragement. He did. The Scripture was, 'Do not judge according to appearance, but judge with righteous judgment' (John 7:24).

"When I got home, the registrar called. There was an opening. *God opened a door.* How I praised the Lord for the wonderful ways He works."

Eighth, thank Him for what He is teaching you.

Take time to review what God has been doing in your

life in this crucial area of time management. You will be greatly encouraged in your God-confidence.

The horrifying morning of the earthquake was only one of many days this year when God himself has shaken up my plans and my goals. Learning to give up MY goals and MY plans, and submit to HIS goals and plans for the day requires a continual attitude adjustment on my part. This is only possible as I learn to accept the absolute control of my sovereign God and thank Him for what He is doing— even though I may not understand what it is, or how what He is doing can possibly be better than my logical plan for a wonderful day of happy accomplishment.

Ask yourself how the Lord is teaching you to apply these *Twelve Time Management Tips* for women of God-confidence:

1. Pray about every single thing. Pray through the day as you breathe.
2. Ask the Lord to teach you time management skills that are personalized for your life and responsibilities, and that are according to His will. "Teach me to do Your will" (Psalm 143:10).
3. Ask the Lord for the wisdom to say *yes*.
4. Ask the Lord for the courage to say *no*.
5. Learn to wait on the Lord for direction.
6. Ask the time management question throughout the day, "What is the best use of my time right now?"
7. Avoid the tyranny of the telephone. Be the master of the telephone, not its slave.
8. Realize that God never asks, expects, or wants you to "do it all!"
9. Ask the Lord for the wisdom to discern if a *yes* answer to a responsibility is people-pressured or God-directed.
10. Evaluate your progress frequently. When you feel breathless, rushed, or harried, ask the Lord to help you to either get out of the "busyness" you're into,

or ask Him to help you get through it with a good attitude!
11. Use this gracious response with friends when necessary: "I can't give you the time you deserve right now."
12. Focus on the Lord throughout each day.

Ninth, don't be discouraged when you "blow it again!"
Erika, one of my daughter's friends, shares a favorite poem. I know it will bless and encourage you as it has so many others:

The Difference

I got up early one morning
and rushed right into the day;
I had so much to accomplish
that I didn't have time to pray.
Problems just tumbled about me
and heavier came each task;
Why doesn't God help me? I wondered.
He said, "But you didn't ask."
I wanted to see joy and beauty
but the day toiled on, gray and bleak;
I wondered why God didn't show me.
He said, "But you didn't seek."
I tried to come into God's presence;
I used all my keys at the lock.
God gently and lovingly chided
"My child, you didn't knock."
I woke up early this morning
And paused before entering the day.
I had so much to accomplish
That I had to take time to pray.
  —Author Unknown

Finally, "M&M"—*Memorize and Meditate*.
If you are to become a woman of God-confidence, you will be memorizing God's Word and meditating on the verses you have learned throughout the day.
Let's review the key verses from this chapter:

"I am the Lord. I do not change" (Malachi 3:6).

"Is anything too hard for the Lord? There is nothing too hard for You" (Genesis 18:14; Jeremiah 32:17, 27).

Pastor Eric: Micah 6:8—"And what does the Lord require of you but to do justly, to love mercy, and to walk humbly with your God?"

Pat: James 5:16—"The effective, fervent prayer of a righteous man (or woman) avails much."

Psalm 118:24—"This is the day which the Lord has made; we will rejoice and be glad in it."

Colossians 3:23—"Whatever you do, do it heartily, as to the Lord and not to men."

Jeanne: Proverbs 3:5–6—"Trust in the Lord with all your heart, and lean not on your own understanding; in all your ways acknowledge Him, and He shall direct your paths."

Isaiah 40:31—"But those who wait on the Lord shall renew their strength; they shall mount up with wings like eagles, they will run and not be weary, they will walk and not faint."

John 7:24—"Do not judge according to appearance, but judge with righteous judgment."

Psalm 143:10—"Teach me to do Your will."

Reflections

1. What are your three biggest time management frustrations?

_____

_____

_____

2. What's going on when you have the least amount of control of your time?

_____

_____

Give an example of a time when you have led a people-pressured life rather than a God-directed life. What were the results?

_____

_____

_____

4. Is your prayer life more like breathing or panic? Why?

_____

_____

_____

5. When is the telephone a time management problem for you?

_____

_____

_____

6. Give two examples of times when you could have used Pastor Eric's "I can't give you the time you deserve right now." When do you plan to use it in the future?

_____

_____

_____

_____

7. How can you adjust your life to make more space for God? Please be specific.

_____

_____

_____

_____

8. Dr. O. Hallesby suggests, "The carnal mind will always instinctively and automatically mobilize every possible reason it can possibly conceive of for not praying at a particular time. For example, you are too busy; your mind is too preoccupied; your heart is not inclined toward prayer; later on you will have more time, your mind will be more calm and collected, and you will be able to pray in a more devotional frame of mind. Before we know it, the entire day is gone, and we have not had a single quiet hour alone with Christ."
Please consider how this applies to your own situation.

9. Carefully review each of the *Twelve Time Management Tips for Women of God-Confidence.* How will each of these help you in the future?

_____

_____

_____

_____

_____

_____

10. Please write a personal comment on each of the ten steps to God-confidence in the area of Time Management.

_____

_____

_____

_____

_____

_____

_____

_____

_____

11. Select one or more verses for your own personal "M&M." Please write them down.

_____

_____

_____

_____

_____

_____

_____

_____

12. After you have committed the first verse to heart, and are beginning to think about it during the day, explain how God is using it in your life.

_____

_____

_____

_____

_____

"With All I Have to Do, I Can Never Feel Finished."

_____

_____

_____

_____

_____

Myth Eight

Dearest heavenly Father—The men in my life can disappoint me so much of the time. I try so hard to make them understand where I'm coming from, to make them understand what I'm thinking and feeling, but I often feel like I'm just wasting my time and my breath. I don't think I'm asking for too much. I just want to be loved and appreciated.

The truth is, men can just drive me crazy! Why is it that in spite of the fact they are so irritating and so frustrating, I long for their approval? Even when I want to give up caring, I can't. Why do I care so much? Why does it seem that I love them more than they love me? Why are they so insensitive to my needs? Why do they withdraw just when I need them most? Why can't I stop caring what they think?

"I Can't Feel Good About Myself Without the Help of the Men in My Life."

IF YOU HAVE EVER LOVED A MAN, the chances are almost 100 percent that you have experienced the quaking and shaking that rumbles through a male-female relationship. It is also nearly 100 percent guaranteed that you have felt like a yo-yo at some time in the relationship. The Male-Female "Self-Esteem" Yo-Yo works like this:

P	and	D
U		O
		W
		N

"I think he likes me."	"I don't think he even knows I exist!"
"I think he likes the way I look."	"He didn't say one thing about how good I looked."
"I think he understands."	"He's the most insensitive man I've ever met."
"I think he's starting to see things my way."	"He's the most perverse, bullheaded, stubborn mule of a man who ever lived!"
"I think he likes it."	"I can never tell what he's thinking. There's no way to please him. If only he'd talk to me."

"I think he must be planning something special for the two of us."

"We almost never go anywhere or do anything together anymore. I'm fed up."

——— ✑ ———

The "Perfect" Man

In the perfection of the Garden of Eden, Eve never wondered. Eve never had to guess. You and I know that Adam was perfect.

He was always interested, could not hear enough of her talk, never interrupted, never rolled his eyes—and never left the room physically or mentally when she was mid-sentence! He was available and supportive. He always took Eve's side in any discussion. He never forgot the day they met, or what she was not wearing. He even remembered exactly what she cooked for their first meal. If the Garden got dusty, Adam was the first to lunge for the Dust Buster.

Romance could have been Adam's middle name! He thrived on planning romantic rendezvous for the two of them. Of course Adam was a brilliant businessman, and Eve's financial future was secure. The mortgage on the Garden was paid off, and the two of them led a debt-free existence. Yet there was plenty of everything everywhere!

Then—*sin* entered.

Everything changed. Slowly at first, but Eve knew. Her first big clue came at the hearing with the Lord! It was a time of great awe and soul searching. Eve was fearful. So was her hero. She had never seen Adam scared before, and it caused her to become even more frightened.

First the Lord questioned Adam. The Lord God asked three questions. It was Adam's answer to the third one that really grabbed Eve. God asked, "Have you eaten from the tree of which I commanded you that you should not eat?" (Genesis 3:11). Adam's response shocked Eve to the core.

"The woman whom You gave to be with me, she gave me of the tree, and I ate."

That's when the internationally popular *Blame Game* began. . . .

And it has been played with great male-female gusto ever since!

This game is a particular favorite of the married set. Peter Feldner gives this heartrending description: "Married fights are different than nonmarried fights. Nonmarried fights are NFL preseason games. You try to win, but you don't want anyone to get hurt. Married fights are civil wars. You win at all costs, and if you can't win, you inflict as many casualties on the enemy as possible before you die."[1]

Perhaps nothing can destroy a woman's fragile bubble of esteem faster than a man. He can be a father, a brother, a friend, a husband. Even a mere male acquaintance or complete stranger can devastate us on any given day with the "wrong" look or the "wrong" word. Worse yet can be that man who simply ignores us when we need to be recognized!

Do you ever wonder why women have this almost uncontrollable craving for the admiration, attention, and love of men? Why, in spite of a woman's best efforts to "never let a man get the best of me again," are many women magnetically drawn back to hoping for their approval over and over again? No matter how severe the hurt and rejection, a woman will continue to struggle for the acceptance of men. Why?

The Man Trap

The answer is as old as that devastating confrontation in Eden. After the Lord patiently questioned Adam and Eve, He pronounced the consequences. To Eve, the Almighty said, "I will greatly multiply your sorrow and your conception. In pain you shall bring forth children; your desire shall be for your husband, and he shall rule over you."

Francis Schaeffer explains it this way. "There are two parts here: the first relates to the womanness of the woman—the bearing of children—and the second to her relationship to her husband. In regard to the former, God says that He will multiply two things—not just the pain but also the conception. It seems clear that if man had not rebelled there would not have been as many children born.

"In regard to the relationship to her husband, God says, 'Your desire shall be for your husband, and he shall rule over you.' This one sentence puts an end to any pure democracy. In a fallen world pure democracy is not possible. Rather, God brings structure into the primary relationship of man—the man-woman relationship. In a fallen world (in every kind of society—big and small—and in every relationship) structure is needed for order. God himself imposes it on the basic human relationship."[2]

Other Bible scholars help us to understand the psychological dependence of women on men that is implicit in the second part of the consequence to Eve's disobedience. "Her reward for this (disobedience) is the almost morbid and continual desire she should experience toward the man in spite of the perils and pains of childbirth, that natural attraction that will not let her free herself from him, the weak dependence that impels her to lean upon the man, and to let herself be sheltered and completed by him. . . . The woman will henceforth involuntarily follow the leading of the man, and be subject even against her will to his dominion."[3]

Another theologian makes this graphic statement: "Besides this bodily suffering on the part of woman, there is to arise psycho-emotional complications for her in her interpersonal relations with the man. Eve had influenced Adam to eat with her, persuading him to do what she wished; she gave to him and he ate with her. Now, she herself finds the psychological balance overturned against her; she will find within herself a yearning for man which on occasion amounts to nymphomania."[4]

An eminent biblical scholar adds, "And kindred to

these pangs of her corporeal frame are the other varied sorrows which overshadow her lot—the weakness, the dependence, the fear, the rising and sinking of heart, the bitterness of disappointed hope, the wounds of unrequited affection."[5]

A renowned theologian explains, "A woman has such an immense psychological dependence on man that she is willing to submit to what is often the man's insensitive and tyrannical rule within marriage. . . . Certainly a woman does submit to sexual intercourse in spite of the known pain of childbearing, in most cases desiring it. There is also a psychological dependence of women on men that many acknowledge, even in this age of increased female self-consciousness.

"A male writer must be careful in what he says in dealing with a subject that often provokes extreme reactions. But it is worth noting that in one contemporary novel dealing with woman's liberation, *The Women's Room*, a character who has been deeply hurt by men and is now trying to make an independent life for herself observes to a friend in the same situation that although they have been hurt by men they still spend most of their time talking about them: 'They're still at the center of our conversation,' she says."[6]

These are strong words, but they certainly shed some spiritual light on the plight of women and help us to understand why we are the way we are in our relationships with men.

This inner need we have for men can give men an inordinate amount of control over us. Whether men consciously realize it or not, they generally have the balance of power in relationships with women.

Free

Now, you may be thinking, *None of this is true for me—never has been and never will be! I don't build my life around men!* Only you can know if you are really free from men in the truest sense—free from needing to react critically

177

and defensively, free from the need to attack all the obvious blustering and blundering. *That* kind of freedom.

If that is *true*, and if you are a Christian woman, I am absolutely certain your freedom comes because Jesus Christ is Lord of your life—and you are wisely looking to Him for satisfaction, completion, fulfillment, rather than looking for final approval from a man! A host of Christian women could tell you stories of what happened when they put man on the throne of their lives rather than the Lord. Looking to any man to meet your needs sets you up for enormous disappointment. There is no human being who can compare with Jesus Christ. To keep life in proper perspective, and to avoid the unnecessary heartache and heartbreak that come when a woman sets up a man as the answer to all her wants and needs, the focus must be on God himself. Then we can trust God to do what is best for us.

Marion

Marion is tall and willowy, with strawberry blond hair and serious green eyes. "I know what it is like to put a man ahead of God," she confided. "I was in my late twenties, and a Christian. The Christian men I had dated seemed so dull and unattractive. My desires always seemed to go toward the unsaved. I knew I shouldn't date non-Christians, but I was angry at the Lord for not giving me anyone terrific, and time was passing by. All my friends were getting married. Hardly a month passed without my attending a wedding. I was a bridesmaid at least twelve times, and it was getting to be an ordeal. Each time I asked the Lord, 'Why isn't it me? What's wrong with me? Why won't you let me have a man?'

"My impatience led me to date an unsaved guy. He was great looking, had a wonderful job, super personality. In short, he was Mr. Wonderful. At twenty-nine, I was determined. This was it. I idolized him. There was nothing I wouldn't do for him, and I did it. It was a miracle I didn't get pregnant.

"After about six months, I wrangled a marriage proposal out of him. I knew he wasn't ready, but I did put a lot of pressure on him. He succumbed, and we set the date. My parents are Christians, and totally opposed the marriage. Many of my friends also warned me. I didn't care. I was determined. I was going to be a *Mrs.* before my thirtieth birthday no matter what. My mother told me that her prayer group would be praying night and day for God to stop the marriage. That bothered me a lot. I told her not to pray. I would marry him and lead him to the Lord. I knew that was not what God wanted, but I didn't care.

"The wedding plans were a disaster. My parents would not consent to having anything to do with a marriage they felt was out of God's will. My fiancé was furious with them. There was a terrible confrontation. I had never seen such rage spill out of a human being. That was a warning from God. I ignored it.

"We had a very small wedding, with few people. My church went along with my parents, so only two or three from the church came. I was deeply hurt, but thought, 'So what! I'll be married! I'll show them!'

"What a fool I was. My charming husband's temper began to show on the honeymoon. No matter what I did, I couldn't seem to please him. I had never seen that side of him before. It frightened me. In the months that followed he picked on me. I felt like his live-in scapegoat. At one point he told me, 'You're too stupid to live!' and smacked me across the face. That was the beginning."

Now Marion began to cry as she regretfully continued her story. "He made me believe I really was stupid and always wrong. So I tried harder. Still I did things that made him angry. He began to hit me more often. Bruises were the result. I kept quiet. I was afraid of him. I was so afraid to tell my parents and Christian friends. I could just hear them say, 'We told you so.' I couldn't have endured that on top of everything else.

"I called out to God, begging His forgiveness and release. I confessed I was wrong and had made a terrible mistake. More time passed. My only comfort was talking to the Lord. He was my only friend, my only hope. Since my husband wouldn't let me go to church, I spent time in the Word whenever I could, hanging on to every word for dear life! I told Jesus, 'You are my Rock, you are my Refuge, you are my Strength, you are my All in All. Please help me, dear God.'

"One day I left work early. I was not feeling well. There was a strange car in the driveway, and my husband's car was in the garage. I entered the house and heard noises coming from our bedroom. I knew what was going on, but I didn't know what to do. I was terribly afraid. 'God, help me!' I pleaded silently.

"Just then my husband emerged naked from the bedroom with wine glasses. He saw me, threw down the glasses and attacked me, screaming terrible things. I was terrified. The girl dressed and left while he was beating me. He did not stop until he was too tired to continue. I was a bloody mess. Somehow I got up, got out, and drove to the hospital. My nose was broken, I had a concussion, as well as other injuries.

"I felt more worthless than I ever had in my life. In the hospital, I remember thinking through the haze, *This shouldn't be happening to me. I'm a child of the King.* Little songs like 'Jesus Loves Me' wandered in and out of my head.

"The hospital called my parents. They came. I was humiliated. The love they showed me was wonderful. They wanted me, their prodigal daughter, to come home. I did. When they tried to contact my husband, they could not locate him anywhere. Apparently, he had moved from our rented house to who knows where. I have never seen or heard from him again.

"That was ten years ago. I am now forty years old. The external wounds healed much more rapidly than the internal hurts. It took years for me to recover. Without God, I couldn't have made it.

"After my horrifying marriage, I determined that God would be on the throne in my life, and that no one ever would become an idol in my life, take the place of the Lord, or rule over Him. The verse that I chose to live by is Matthew 6:33: 'But seek first the kingdom of God and His righteousness, and all these things shall be added to you.'

"God has been more than gracious. During the long years of healing, dating was not even an option for me. I was not interested, nor ready. The Lord knew that, so He did not allow anyone to come into my life. It didn't matter. I was content with being single. Two years ago, God gave me His choice of a husband, so much different than the choice I had so foolishly made years ago. I have been married for a little over a year. *Vive la Différence!* My husband and I together 'seek first the kingdom of God and His righteousness.' This time, I let God give me the marriage partner of His choosing."

Norma

Many Christian women suffer in their relationships with men. Little girls are highly vulnerable to abuse, even from fathers who call themselves "Christians." In Chapter 4, you were introduced to Norma and Jayni. Norma is the mother who has been at Jayni's side during her young lifetime of prolonged debilitating illness. Now meet them as victims in the world's eyes, but triumphant through Christ.

Norma looks back over forty years of marriage: "I did not come from a Christian home, but my parents were kind and loving. I met Rudy when I was fifteen. He was eighteen and in the Marine Corps. Right from the start I was madly in love with him. He was charming, handsome, complimentary, and had a very good sense of humor.

"I didn't know a lot about him or his background, just that his parents were divorced. He would come down on weekends from the base and stay with his father. We dated for three years before he asked me to marry him. My parents were not happy that I was going to get married before graduating from high school, but we did marry, and Rudy was sent to Japan. We both wrote faithfully, and I finished high school.

"The second year of our marriage, he was back, and I discovered then that he had a very low opinion of women. He made me feel like he didn't trust me. He was very jealous.

"I had two miscarriages in three years, and he implied that I was not strong enough or woman enough to carry his child. That hurt me very deeply. When I got pregnant again, he was very demanding. He didn't want me to do anything because I might lose the baby. I felt protected but I also felt incapable.

"Rudy would be at the base all week and come home on the weekends. Eventually, he started seeing other women. He did not tell me about it, but I knew.

"I was seven months pregnant with our second child when Rudy called to tell me he was not coming home. He told me he wanted to go to the drag races. Of course, Rudy did not go to the drag races; I found out sometime later that he was with another woman.

"Finally, Rudy told me that he had been sexually molested for years by his mother and by his sister. He also told me that his mother slept with boyfriends in their home while she was still married to his father.

"Then the Lord started bringing Christians into our lives, and eventually we both accepted Jesus Christ as our Savior. We became very active in church and our whole life revolved around the Lord. There were struggles, but Rudy did a complete turn around.

"After I came to the Lord, my confidence grew. I came to feel more worthwhile. I had godly confidence. I could deal with things differently. Although my life continued to be filled with trauma, the Lord gave me much wisdom in many areas.

"When we accepted the Lord, I believe it was a true

commitment on Rudy's part. But then he drew himself away from the Lord because of what he began to do to the children." For the first time in our interview, Norma wept. "I didn't know. I didn't suspect. I can only imagine the turmoil. Rudy was a moody person. As it turned out, all of the children were sexually abused."

Jayni, the youngest, says, "During the abuse, there were so many nights I'd yell at the ceiling. 'Help me Jesus! where are you?' I would wonder why Jesus didn't come. I would wonder why Jesus didn't stop it. I would wonder why He wasn't keeping His promises. All of this evolved into a severe hatred of my dad that lasted until the day he died.

"I flipped into rage at the Lord. But God has been patient with me. I am starting to find comfort and peace. I don't blame Him anymore for what happened. I am seeing a purpose in it. Because I have known so many types of pain, I can experience life more fully and am able to help other people. That gives me joy. James 1:2 and 3 are my verses: 'My brethren, count it all joy when you fall into various trials, knowing that the testing of your faith produces patience.'

"I'm doing pretty well now. I've made it through the worst. My life is growing into something peaceful."

A Message to Other Abused Women

I asked Norma what she would like to say to other wives and mothers who have experienced some of what she has. "First of all, if you have a relationship with the Lord, He will give you the strength to bear up and get you through. If you're lying in bed at night, you will sense that He's there with you. If you're at work, driving in the car, you will sense His presence. He has said that He will 'never leave you nor forsake you' (Hebrews 13:5). I believe that with all my heart.

"Since I lost Rudy, the Lord has become to me the kind of husband that I was denied for so many years. If I didn't live my faith moment by moment, my life would be destroyed. What I want to say to any woman who understands my pain is, 'Get down on your knees right now and cry out to Jesus Christ. The Lord himself is the only One who will get you through if you really trust Him moment by moment.

"I don't know what purpose God has for me in all this. I pray that whatever I say or do will give Him the honor and glory He deserves. I know I have a real peace in my life that I have never had before, even though I've known the Lord for many years. My life is not free of turmoil, but I have 'the peace of God, which surpasses all understanding' (Philippians 4:7). Even though forty years of my life is behind me, I feel like I've got a lot of living to do!"

Believing that without forgiveness, peace is not possible. I asked both Norma and Jayni about their respective stages of forgiveness.

Jayni said, "I'm in process. Because of God, I'm a lot further than I ever thought I'd even want to be. I don't know my dad's heart. It is hard for me to believe he was truly born again."

Then Norma reflects on forgiveness. "I have forgiven Rudy as much as I possibly can at this point. I feel that by the time my life ends, and I go before the Lord, there will be total forgiveness in my heart for Rudy."

Steps to God-Confidence in the Area of Men

First, understand that *strife* is the normal lot of fallen men and women—and our marriages need the Spirit of God as much as our individual souls.

Sometimes we deceive ourselves into thinking that we are "the only one" who is having some form of marital strife, and we are embarrassed to even discuss it with God. You can be assured that because marriage is a union of two imperfect people, there will be problems. Marital conflicts are as certain as death and taxes! God knows. God understands.

You and I must race to our Father to tell Him how we feel, and ask Him for help with our attitudes and actions.

We generally hear of Susanna Wesley in terms of ideal motherhood. Did you know that she had a difficult marriage? She and Samuel had a serious long-term disagreement regarding politics. In utter frustration, she wrote to a close friend, "I am more easy in the thoughts of parting because I think we are not likely to live happily together."[7] How utterly amazing! Particularly when we recall that Susanna Wesley lived in the late 1600s and early 1700s!

Samuel Wesley was not a successful clergyman. "He was appointed to a parish where many Nonconformist families lived, and tensions grew between the pastor and some members of his reluctant congregation.

"Many nights, mobs surrounded the Wesley parsonage, beating drums, firing guns in the air, and pelting the house with stones. The local congregation refused to pay his salary.

"Members of his own congregation had him arrested and sent to a debtor's prison, leaving Susanna and the children with only thirty shillings.

"Now in those days, food was not provided to prisoners by the state; if they were to eat, it was up to their families to provide food at the jail. Susanna proposed to her husband that she sell her wedding ring in order to buy his food while he was in jail; but he preferred to go hungry rather than have her sell her only earthly treasure."[8]

Susanna trusted the Lord for help and sought His guidance and comfort. She knew there was no earthly support. Over time this Christian heroine of strong faith resolved her marital problems with the Lord, and was able to write to her brother, "He is not fit for worldly business, but where he lives I will live, and where he dies I will die, and there will I be buried."[9]

When Samuel died, Susanna was left penniless and homeless. Although grinding poverty and back-breaking work punctuated her life on earth, at the end she was able to exult, "All my sufferings . . . have concurred to promote my spiritual and eternal good. . . . Glory be to Thee, O Lord!"[10]

Yes, strife may be our natural lot—but in Christ, with the Lord as our true husband, we can have an unsurpassed *peace* and *confidence*, no matter what.

Second—face the fact that when it comes to men, we can tend to get our focus off of God. We either compete with, mother, or depend on them. By losing our God-focus, men take the place of importance that only God should have, becoming idols in our lives. Then we are consigned to a cycle of disappointment, hurt, anger, and humiliation.

Melanie is a soft-spoken, sensitive brunette with blue eyes. She knows what it is like to have life crash apart at a very young age. "I was going into the tenth grade, and went to a slumber party at a girlfriend's. She had an older brother who was already out of school. He came home while we were in the living room. Most of the girls were asleep. He motioned for me to come into his room with him. I didn't think it was any big deal.

"Before I knew it, he had me on the floor. I didn't scream because I thought his parents would blame me. When it was over, he walked me down the hall and left me at the bathroom. I don't remember him saying anything.

"The next morning I walked home, three houses away. My mother took one look at me and knew something was wrong. I told her what happened. My father confronted him, but I refused to go through the court system. I never saw him again. My parents sold the house and we moved across town.

"I knew the Lord at this time, but I was not a strong Christian. I didn't blame God and I didn't turn to Him. I voided everything out. I went to a rape crisis center but don't remember one thing.

"I felt like he had taken away from me something I could never get back. I was extremely emotional after the rape. I took everything very personally. A year later I became suicidal. I had pills at school but was stopped.

"When I turned sixteen, I fell in with a group of kids

that were into drugs. I wanted acceptance, and I got into it too. I wanted every boy I went with to be the one who would finalize things and make it last forever.

"I began to suspect I was pregnant. I told my mother something was wrong. She took me to the doctor. It was positive. She gave me no choice as to what was going to happen next. The pregnancy was terminated the next morning. She never mentioned it again.

"I was numb. It was all so fast. I didn't have time to feel. There was no one to talk to about it. My mother wouldn't talk to me. When I told my boyfriend he didn't say anything that I remember, and he already had another girl-friend.

"Through all of this I was a regular church attender, but I wasn't grounded in the Lord. Today, I am a strong Christian.

"I claim Romans 8:28 as my verse: 'And we know that all things work together for good to those who love God, to those who are the called according to His purpose.'

"The abortion still haunts me. I was told the baby was a cell, and nothing more. When I became older, I found this wasn't true. It took me a long time to feel forgiven. But now I have laid it all at the cross and I know I am forgiven.

"I can actually thank God for what I've been through because I know He will use it to help someone else.

"And I've forgiven my mother too. She wasn't a real strong Christian at that time. She was trying to protect me as best she could. And in spite of what she made me do, she's all against abortion now. She goes to the rallies and holds up signs. She's very involved. I think it's her way of dealing with the guilt.

"Now, because I know I am weak I look to the Lord for strength."

No matter how wonderful you may imagine a man to be, the truth is no man on earth can love you or me the way we need or want to be loved. Reality will always disappoint the fantasy. Male human flesh will fail. He's a mere mortal, with tons if imperfections . . . just like us.

God doesn't want us to experience the disappointment, rejection, heartbreak, grief, or devastating humiliation that putting a male idol on the throne of our lives will cause. That's why He warns us all through His Word to keep away from creating idols. The only way to save ourselves from the heartbreak and pain a man can cause is to keep God on the throne of our lives. A woman must never let a man become more important in her life than God. Only Jesus Christ never disappoints or disillusions.

Third, be aware that it is only when we "give up"— knowing all our manipulations and all attempts to please have failed—that God can begin to do a wonderful work in our relationships with men.

Diana is an artist. "I march to a different drummer . . . but that rebellious march got me into trouble because I was determined to do it *my way.*

"I've always loved men. In fact, I've always preferred them to women. I just want to be completely honest.

"I started dating early and had a huge amount of fun. I was careful not to lose my head, and I didn't want to lose my heart either—not until Mr. Right walked into my life.

"After a long struggle with finding out about God and what Jesus did for me on the cross, I yielded myself to Him, confessed my many sins, and accepted Him as my Savior and Lord. Then I waited, expecting that the Lord would send Mr. Right rushing into my life.

"The Lord was moving too slowly for my taste, so I decided I would just have to take matters into my own hands. Soon I met a guy whom I liked a lot. He appreciated my artwork and knew quite a bit about art. We had so much fun together. I laughed more when I was with him than with anyone I'd ever known. I used to tell him that being with him was 'Laugh Therapy.'

"Was he a Christian? Nope! But he was so nice, and so good. He believed in God, so I thought in a little while Jesus would be important to him too.

"Wrong! But by this time I was really in love. How I *rationalized* our relationship. I kidded myself into believing I was this great witness to him. I was such a great witness that I moved into his neat apartment and we set up housekeeping. I was certain we were moving toward marriage. But he wasn't. He was very pleased with our arrangement and didn't want to foul it up with marriage. This was fine for a while, because I was certain I would prevail. Months went by. He did not even want to discuss marriage. It was the one black cloud in our relationship. That, and the fact I was living with a non-believer.

"At this point, he had an opportunity for a job in Paris and wanted me to go along. I could not pack fast enough. If he wanted me in Paris, he wanted me to be his bride. Wrong again! No proposal in Paris, no marriage in France.

"God was not through with me. Now the Lord began to convict me of my sin. Down deep I knew that this man was not ever planning to marry me. That pierced me. I loved him so much. Just thinking about leaving him gave me a heartache and a hollow pit in my stomach. I did not believe I could live without him. I didn't believe life would be worth living without him. Everything was still perfect, except for the fact that he would not marry me.

"After two years of ridiculous ultimatums I couldn't follow through on, I made the most difficult decision of my life. It was the Lord who gave me strength. I left him. I returned to the U.S. alone at thirty-two years old.

"He wrote to me. I forced myself not to write. I was heartbroken. There could never be a man like him ever. He was my once in a lifetime. He begged me to return. But now I was back in the Word, back in church, with Christian friends who were praying for me. That's what made it bearable. The verses I would repeat over and over again were Proverbs 3:5–6: 'Trust in the Lord with all your heart, and lean not on your own understanding; in all your ways acknowledge him, and he shall direct your paths.'

"One year went by. He called on my birthday and said that he wanted me to know he had started reading the Bible because he knew it had meant a lot to me, and reading it made him less lonely for me.

"I was determined to leave it entirely up to God.

"Another full year went by. I wasn't dating. I didn't even want to. I knew he was the only man I would ever love, but I wanted to obey the Lord, and trust Him to 'give me the desires of my heart,' even though I wasn't too sure what it all meant.

"He called and asked me to call him. He said he had some wonderful news. My mouth was dry, and my hands were shaking as I dialed the number. He wasn't there! I kept calling. I did not reach him for several hours. Then he told me the news: He had accepted Jesus Christ as his Savior. I have never felt such emotion. I just wept and wept. He told me the wonderful way the Lord had used His Word to bring him to himself.

"But that wasn't all that happened. He asked me to marry him! After all the years, and all the tears! I cried some more. I had long since given up all hope, knowing my dream would never come true. But it did, in the most incredible way possible.

"What I want to say to other women like me is simply 'give up and trust the Lord.' That's it! That's all."

God does not usually give a woman the man that she picked out for herself and lived with in an unmarried situation. But God can do anything, anywhere, at any time! In this case, God allowed them to meet, to be together, to part, to provide enough time for Diana to get her relationship with Him as her primary focus, and lead the man to a saving knowledge of himself. Then, and only then, could God put them back together in a most beautiful and romantic way! Remember: God created romance. However, when we plot, plan, and manipulate, the romance goes rotten. In this case, it was only the power of the Holy Spirit working in both lives that was able to restore and renew the broken relationship!

Fourth, if you are single, believe that God knows what's best for you, and that He cares more about your joy, contentment, and fulfillment than you do. God delights in doing good things for His people when they trust, obey, and learn to wait for His best.

While I was growing up I remember my mother telling this lovely story. I always think of it when women are becoming "desperate" in their desire for a man, and think all hope is gone. I asked her to repeat it once more to encourage and bless you also.

"I was young at the time, and Tallah seemed terribly old. She had to be over forty. She had gray hair, a thin face, and terrible teeth. She was anything but beautiful. Because of some impediment, she had to have a specially built shoe that came above her ankle. Even with it, she walked with a limp and a cane.

"We lived down the street. Her mother and sister treated her like Cinderella. She did all the cooking and cleaning. I think all they did was complain. Our family had nothing to do with the mother and sister.

"Tallah sang in the choir in our little corner church. I know the only qualification for choir membership was the ability to walk to the choir loft.

"A very nice fellow from Amarillo with a Texas twang came to visit the church. He was moving to the area. I know he had to be at least five or ten years younger than Tallah.

"He joined the choir, and as time went by he became interested in Tallah and then wanted to marry her. It had to be God. Naturally, her domineering mother and sister were against it. They didn't want to lose their live-in help! But everyone in the church was one hundred percent for the marriage.

"They did marry and he was very good to her. They had a nice-looking daughter. I was always impressed with the devotion of this man to his handicapped wife. They had a wonderful marriage."

Fifth, remember that God is *omnipotent* and *omniscient*. He alone can change the men in our lives in His way, in His time, and for His purposes. Even if you are married to a man who is opposed to your Christian beliefs—*pray* and *trust*.

Dr. M. Lon Kasow is a well-known and much respected eye doctor. He was raised an Orthodox Jew, and pursued rabbinical studies. "I was always seeking God," Dr. Kasow recalls. "Something was missing in the synagogue, though, and I decided to leave the rabbinical studies and enlist in the army, even though I had an exemption. The rabbi was furious.

"I continued to seek God. I was trying to find an answer to the things that seemed to be missing from my life. I married Harriet. We had a wonderful marriage, with two beautiful children. Neither of us even raised our voices at each other. Still something was missing.

"I became acquainted with a Catholic woman. One day I asked, 'How come Catholics hate Jews?' She was aghast. 'How can you say that when Jesus was a Jew?' That blew my mind. The door of my spiritual mind began to open.

"I read the Scriptures with a renewed passion. God was speaking to me, of this I was certain. After seeing a painting of the Crown of Thorns, I realized what Jesus Christ had done for me, Lon Kasow, on Calvary. So great was my vision of this that I was literally caught up for three days, consumed by the Lord's total life leading to Calvary. I gave my heart and life to my precious Lord.

"I had been married for twenty-two years. Several times I attempted to speak to Harriet about my new life. I asked her questions. She suggested I go to a psychologist, a psychiatrist, or a rabbi for help. I dropped the subject.

"Later I told her, 'I'm going to be baptized.' She was stunned and told me firmly, 'If you get baptized, I will divorce you.' I got baptized. She divorced me. I was brokenhearted when she left. I was still trying to understand and to make sense of all that had happened.

"As the years passed, Harriet and I never lost communication with each other. It wasn't just the children, we cared for each other. Harriet always said, 'If I remarry, Lon, it will need to be someone just like you.'

"Harriet did remarry, and so did I. Neither of us had more children. Our second spouses died several years ago. I thought to myself, *I would love to marry Harriet again, but only on the condition that she accept the Lord Jesus Christ as her personal Savior.*

"There has been miracle after miracle after miracle. Harriet did come to the Lord. *Hallelujah!* We had been married for twenty-two years—and after a twenty-two-year break, we were remarried by a messianic rabbi who has come to know the Lord. Our children stood up for us, and our grandchildren were the ringbearers and flower girls. The church that we attend is a fellowship of Jewish believers.

"I am amazed at who Jesus is and how He works!"

Sixth, trust God to do wonderful things for you in your relationship with men, and He will do it as you learn to seek Him first. God does bring "beauty for ashes," and He does give the "oil of joy for mourning" (Isaiah 61:3) in relationships with men. Forgiveness is crucial!

No, God does not wave a magic wand and "make it all better." It involves our choosing.

We can choose to be miserable and do things our own way and in our own strength until the day we die. Or we can choose to yield to God for help for each and every personal need.

Life is about choice—and there will be consequences. You've been reading about some of them. You've heard of others. Some of the consequences are great, some are dreadful. For every action on your part with a man, there is, and always will be, a reaction.

Robert Louis Stevenson spoke these riveting words of truth: "Everyone, sooner or later, sits down to his banquet of consequences."

Just today I had lunch with a Christian woman whose family I've known for over twenty years. She will not forgive her Christian husband for a business failure—and yet he has been steadily employed for almost all of their twenty-five years of marriage. She will not forgive him for adultery, which he confessed to her without her having to discover it. She will not forgive him for fondling a foster child. He admitted this, has been forgiven by the foster child, the rest of the children, and has sought help. But most of all, she will not forgive him for becoming the man she wanted to make him into when they got married!

She insists on hanging on to her grievances—using them like a weapon of control. This lack of forgiveness has sabotaged the marriage and is alienating the children. They side with their father, who has admitted the mistakes to himself, to God, to them, and is taking responsible measures for correction.

The children shudder in remembrance of the verbal abuse the mother has hurled at the father year after year. One of the grown children confided, "I couldn't wait to get out of the house. My mother just became unglued too often. She would have screaming fits. It would start out with one of us, and then really get going with my dad. She would scream for hours. Sometimes I had a hard time sleeping. I couldn't take it any longer. I'm glad I was old enough to leave. I feel sorry for my dad and the younger kids."

The children are amazed that their dad remains in the home married to her. He simply says, "I know I've been wrong. I've made a lot of mistakes. With God's help, I'm working on them. I love my wife, and I want to be in the home with my children."

I asked the man if he had hope. "I have to believe there is hope. I cling to God with that hope. She threatens divorce frequently. Sometimes I'm ready to give up, and then God gives me a hopeful sign. In spite of everything my wife has said and done, I believe she loves me more than she knows. God has given me a love for her."

She and I have had long talks through the years about the children and about her husband. We are very good friends. There is nothing we haven't talked about, and no honest word of counsel I've omitted. The words I hear most often from her are, "I know, but . . ."

She's made her choice: to be in control rather than let-ting go of her hurt and anger, and letting God heal, restore, and make something beautiful out of the marriage.

Another Christian woman I know was an uncontrolla-ble screamer. Instead of seeking wise counsel, and learn-ing to change, she was defensive about her actions and ac-cusing of her Christian husband. Sure her husband had faults. Don't they all? Sure she got disgusted and disgrun-tled. Don't we all? She chose to play the *Blame Game*.

After more than twenty years, he left. The elders of the church went to him. His response was horrifying. "I'd rather go to hell than go back to that woman!" He really believed that it was hell on earth to live with a screaming, controlling woman who would not seek the help she so desperately needed. The children and the husband knew she was crying for help; so did her friends. Everyone told her. But—the choice was hers. She chose to ignore every-one.

When he left, she was stunned and bereft. "I never thought he'd go. I never thought he'd really do it!" She would like to have him back, and now, for the first time, she is beginning to assume some of the responsibility for what happened. Because she has stopped playing the in-famous *Blame Game*, and is casting all her cares on the Lord in seeking help and healing, there can be hope.

Naturally healing, forgiveness, and restoration take a long time—a very long time! Our attitudes and actions have been learned over a period of years. Even with an ear-nest desire to change, and with the help of God himself, it takes time, energy, and special self-awareness to change behavior patterns. You must be patient—with yourself, with others.

Ruth Bell Graham has made this profound comment: "A good marriage is the union of two forgivers!" Never have truer words been spoken!

Having a man on the throne of your life, as your idol, can also work in a negative way as we have seen with both of these women. What each did not realize is that, in blaming the husband for everything, the man becomes the total focus, the consuming passion, the total control. The man becomes a dark god—an idol. The man is on the throne of the life, rather than God, even though it is in a negative way. The man is still controlling every single thought.

Playing *Blame Game* with this amount of negative passion is like having a transfusion of poison going through the blood stream night and day. It will spell D-E-A-T-H to the marital relationship, and D-E-S-T-R-U-C-T-I-O-N to the family. The children will absorb the poison and inject it into their relationships with the parents, with each other, and with friends.

Do you see why God hates idolatry so much? God knows that nothing good will ever come when we allow someone else to come between us and Him. God wants us to live lives of joy and peace. Whenever a woman is consumed by a man, peace and joy are replaced by anxiety and moodiness.

Seventh, look for changes and thank God. Remember that your attitude and behavior need changing first. Then God, by the transforming power of His Holy Spirit, will be able to do incredible and unbelievable things in your relationships with men.

The book entitled *Stepping Heavenward* was first published in 1869. It is the charming journal of a nineteenth-century girl. It has twentieth-century honesty and reality. There are two entries, written ten years apart, I would like to share with you.

"February 15—Our honeymoon ends today. There hasn't been quite as much honey in it as I expected. I supposed that Ernest would be at home every evening, at least, and that he would read aloud, and have me play and sing, and that we would have delightful times together. But now that he has got me, he seems satisfied, and goes about his business as if he had been married a hundred years. In the morning he goes off to see his list of patients; he is going in and out all day; after dinner we sit down to have a nice talk together, the doorbell rings, and he is called away.

Then in the evening he goes and sits in his office and studies; I don't mean every minute, but he certainly spends hours there. Today he brought me such a precious letter from dear Mother! I could not help crying when I read it, it was so kind and loving. Earnest looked amazed; he threw down his paper, came and took me in his arms and asked, 'What is the matter, darling?' Then it all came out. I said I was lonely, and hadn't been used to spending my evenings all by myself.

" 'You must get some of your friends to come and see you, poor child,' he said.

" 'I don't want friends,' I sobbed out. 'I want you.'

" 'Yes, darling; why didn't you tell me so sooner? Of course I will stay with you if you wish it.

" 'If that is your only reason, I am sure I don't want you,' I pouted.

"He looked puzzled.

" 'I really don't know what to do,' he said, with a most comical look of perplexity. But he went to his office, and brought up a pile of musty old books.

" 'Now, dear,' he said, 'we understand each other, I think. I can read here just as well as downstairs. Get your book and we shall be as cozy as possible.'

"My heart felt sore and dissatisfied. Am I unreasonable and childish? What is married life? An occasional meeting, a kiss here and a caress there? Or is it the sacred union of two lovers who walk together side by side, knowing each other's joys and sorrows, and going heavenward hand in hand?[11]

After ten years of marriage, a young woman asked her for advice. "Tell me how I can be sure that if I love a man I shall go on loving him through all the wear and tear of married life, and how can I be sure he can and will go on loving me?"[12]

Her response is as appropriate for us today as it was over 100 years ago.

"Happiness, in other words, love, in married life is not a mere accident. When the union has been formed, as most

Christian unions are, by God himself, it is His intention and His will that it shall prove the unspeakable joy of both husband and wife, and become more and more so from year to year.

"But we are imperfect creatures, wayward and foolish as little children, horribly unreasonable, selfish, and willful. We are not capable of enduring the shock of finding at every turn that our idol is made of clay, and that it is prone to tumble off its pedestal and lie in the dust, till we pick it up and set it in its place again.

"I was struck with Ernest's asking in the very first prayer he offered in my presence, after our marriage, that God would help us love each other. I felt that love was the very foundation on which I was built, and that there was no danger that I would ever fall short in giving to my husband all he wanted, in full measure. But as he went on day after day repeating this prayer, and I naturally made it with him, I came to see that this most precious of earthly blessings had been and must be God's gift, and that while we both looked at it in that light, and felt our dependence on Him for it, we might safely encounter together all the assaults made upon us by the world, the flesh, and the devil.

"I believe we owe it to this constant prayer that we have loved each other so uniformly and with such growing comfort in each other; so that our little discords always have ended in fresh accord, and our love has felt conscious of resting on a rock—and that rock was the will of God."[13]

Camille, a mom and wife who knows how to prayerfully handle the many problems in her life, told me one day, "Every day my husband and I pray together, we get along. Every day we do not pray together, we do not get along!" It could never be said better in fewer words!

Elizabeth Prentiss is the woman who wrote the journal entries. She also wrote the beautiful hymn, "More Love to Thee," which is an ideal prayer for each of us to sing as we proceed on our upward journey toward increasing God-confidence:

More love to Thee, O Christ, more love to Thee!
Hear thou the prayer I make on bended knee;
This is my earnest plea:
More love, O Christ, to Thee,
More love to Thee, more love to Thee!
Once earthly joy I craved, sought peace and rest;
Now Thee alone I seek—give what is best:
This all my prayer shall be:
More love, O Christ, to Thee,
More love to Thee, more love to Thee![14]

Eighth, "M&M"—*Memorize and Mediate*.

The verses in this chapter are jewels, meant to bless and encourage you:

Marion: Matthew 6:33—"But seek first the kingdom of God and His righteousness, and all these things shall be added to you."

Norma: Hebrews 13:5—"I will never leave you nor forsake you."

Philippians 4:7—"And the peace of God, which surpasses all understanding, will guard your hearts and minds through Christ Jesus."

Jayni: James 1:2–3—"Count it all joy when you fall into various trials, knowing that the testing of your faith produces patience."

Melanie: Romans 8:28—"And we know that all things work together for good to those who love God, to those who are the called according to His purpose."

2 Corinthians 12:9—"My grace is sufficient for you, for my strength is made perfect in weakness."

Diana: Proverbs 3:5–6—"Trust in the Lord with all your heart, and lean not on your own understanding; in all your ways acknowledge Him, and He shall direct your paths."

Each woman: Isaiah 61:3—"To give them beauty for ashes, the oil of joy for mourning, the garment of praise for the spirit of heaviness . . . that He may be glorified."

Reflections

1. In your relationships with men, what are the three biggest problem areas?

_____

_____

_____

2. Has the *Male-Female "Self-Esteem" Yo-Yo* operated in your life? If so, how?

_____

_____

3. Do any of the men in your life play the *Blame Game*? Do you? If so, when are you most likely to get involved with it?

_____

_____

_____

_____

4. Comment on the female psychological dependence on men that is recognized by people as diverse as the female writer of a book on women's lib and biblical scholars.

_____

_____

_____

_____

5. Of the stories shared in this chapter, which affected you most deeply? Please explain, and relate it to your own situation.

_____

_____

_____

_____

_____

_____

6. Have you or anyone you know ever made a man into an idol?

_____

_____

7. Write a personal comment on each of the eight steps to God-confidence in the area of relationships with men.

_____

_____

_____

_____

_____

_____

8. Select one or more verses for your own personal "M&M." Write them down here.

_____

_____

_____

_____

_____

_____

_____

_____

_____

_____

_____

_____

_____

9. After you have committed the first verse to memory, and are beginning to meditate on it during your waking hours, explain how God is making it real in your life.

_____

_____

_____

_____

_____

_____

_____

_____

Date of response_____.

Myth Nine

Dearest heavenly Father, other Christians can be so cruel. Why is it that they can't wait to find fault, to criticize? Some of them remind me of animals ready to pounce on the first prey that comes by. This time it was me.

Dear God, sometimes I wake at night with my heart pounding, and I can scarcely breathe just thinking about what they have done to me with their vicious words and accusations. Please come to my rescue. You are the only one who understands. You are my only hope of deliverance, Father!

"My Christian Friends Would Never Hurt Me."

GROWING UP, I REMEMBER HEARING Dr. J. Vernon McGee quote this little ditty:

To dwell above with saints we love,
Ah! That will be glory.
To live below with saints we know,
Well, that's a different story!

Isn't that the truth? There are a lot of Christians who are really tough to get along with. "Gritty" people are sprinkled through Christendom like sand at the seashore. Like tiny irritating grains they turn up everywhere and get into everything!

Anyone who has known the Lord for any length of time has experienced the trauma of being offended by fellow believers. If it hasn't happened to you, it will—I guarantee it!

In my mind's eye, I see the body of Christ here on earth as covered with self-inflicted wounds. Some of the wounds are superficial, others are deep and festering. There are scars on this body. Yes, there have been wounds, but they have healed. In some cases, the scars are barely visible. In other cases the scars are swollen deformities. There are also many surgical scars.

What determines how well and how quickly a wound to the spirit will be healed? It is the potent factor of *forgiveness*.

Melanie

Melanie, whom you met in Chapter 8, was wounded when she was a young and vulnerable fourteen-year-old. "I came to know the Lord when I was nine. Actually, I was baptized and that was it. How to live the Christian life was never talked about. There were a lot of fun social activities in the church, and I was involved in them.

"When I was fourteen years old, the youth group had a get-together at the pastor's house. There was a seventeen-year-old boy there. We liked each other but hadn't really dated. That night the two of us went to the field next door to smoke. When he tried to have sex with me I started to cry. He stopped and that was the end of it.

"We continued to go to the same church. The following summer at the church camp, he brought a girlfriend. He must have bragged to her about the incident in the field, because she asked me about it. When I told her it was true, she went crazy. She went to him about it and everybody else found out, including his parents.

"When I returned to church, the leaders told me I would have to apologize to the entire congregation. He was told the same thing. He said he wouldn't do it and left the church. I figured that if an adult told me to do something I had to do it.

"I got up in the morning service in front of everyone. They told me I didn't need to go into detail. I was crying. I said, 'I've done something wrong. I'm sorry.' When it was over I kept crying. I couldn't stop.

"I felt so worthless and angry. His parents were there, but they were loving through the whole thing. They didn't think I was the bad person.

"I had no teaching. I didn't think about turning to God. I buried it and tried not to think about it. I forgave everyone involved, but I had a harder time forgiving myself."

Fortunately, Melanie experienced the healing of forgiveness. Sometimes the inexperience of youth gives a resiliency in that area.

Even Christian leaders are not exempt from hurts by other Christians; in fact, their high visibility can make them a natural target for the sword-like tongue of another Christian.

Well-loved Christian humorist Patsy Clairmont candidly shares:

"I hate feeling rejected . . . I like to be liked. . . . So when a platform personality came to me after I spoke at a large event and wanted to chat, I was pleased.

"She was warm and affirming and asked if she could recommend me to groups as she traveled. I was complimented and grateful. We chatted nonstop, then hugged and agreed to meet the following day for another visit before our departure.

"When I met with her the next day, there seemed to be a problem. By her actions I could tell I was it.

"She went from cool to cold to curt. I went from confused to hurt to ticked. The ticked part came afterward, as I tried to figure out how I had fallen from favor. Later, I learned an acquaintance had spent some time with this speaker discussing me. I guess 'Poached Patsy' didn't taste too good, because she certainly seemed to have indigestion.

"The more I thought about the injustice of this encounter, the angrier I became. The incident stirred up memories of every unfair situation I'd ever experienced. I brooded, I boiled, and occasionally I blew up."[1]

Patsy goes on to relate that three years later, she still felt intensely about the incident. "I understand now that the woman's momentary rejection of me was not as damaging as my long-term choice to raise rage."[2]

Being famous and in demand nationally as a speaker does not immunize any Christian woman from the pain of the puncture wound of rejection. It hurts deeply. We don't understand why it happened. We can't comprehend why another Christian would want to listen to lies and believe them. We get frustrated and angry. Peace flies out the door.

Until we make a conscious choice to forgive the person

(or people) who wronged us, we will not experience the beautiful peace and joy of the Lord. And it's difficult. There is so much hurt in the Christian community.

Some years ago I realized the truth of these appalling words: "The Christian army is the only army that shoots its wounded!" It is true that the battlefield of the Christian army is strewn with the mangled bodies of Christian soldiers who have been stabbed in the back, shot in the saddle, blown-up or bulldozed at close range by their own. The crippled are left for dead as the rest of the army goes marching by, singing spiritual songs!

This is certainly not a new phenomenon. "Scripture reveals that even the first-century church experienced inner turmoil and conflict. There were complaints in Jerusalem about what was done with church money. Peter and Paul disagreed about how to treat Gentile converts. Missionary partners Paul and Barnabas split up over whom to take along as an assistant. The Corinthian church divided into warring factions under the banners of their favorite preachers."[3]

We have the same strife today. Just a lot more of it. The names are different. The circumstances have changed, but the backbiting can be brutal. The poet and cynic Lord Byron wrote, "Christians have burnt each other, quite persuaded that all the Apostles would have done as they did."[4]

Hurts can come in reaction to anything and everything. *Money* is a good one. How many Christians do you know who have entrusted their money to someone in the church, only to have it evaporate along with the financial caretaker?

I never knew my father-in-law. He was a postman, and he died when my husband was still young. My mother-in-law scrimped, taught art in her home, and did what she could to provide basic necessities for her four sons. Before her husband died, they purchased a modest home from a Christian in their church, who happened to live next door. Somehow, because of the shenanigans of this Christian, they ended up owing thousands more on the house than was originally agreed. They did not believe in taking fellow believers to court, so they paid the money over a long period of time. "They suffered intense financial strain as a result," their eldest son recalls. "But never in the ten years they lived next door to the people did they utter a harsh word to them about the injustice. They determined to trust the Lord, forgive the people, and treat them with the loving respect they believed Jesus would." He adds this powerful statement. "They also kept their mouths shut. No one in the church knew." My husband is the youngest son, and he didn't even know about it!

I find that very convicting! The phones in Christian homes are often busy as we women discuss, dissect, dismember, disfigure, and nearly destroy other Christians. This can be done under the guise of a "prayer request," or "You need to know about."

I know, because I've been guilty of doing this. It's so easy, particularly if I don't agree with whatever stand the "other" Christian is taking on a particular issue. Sometimes I'm spewing rapid-fire opinions without even knowing the facts. Actually, the fewer facts I have, the more brilliant and incisive my comments can be. Many times, facts just complicate my simple solutions. In record time, I have been responsible for shooting down a fellow believer in a way that would send me racing for comfort if someone were doing the same to me.

After one of my deadly diatribes, I have been convicted of my sin. Yes, I know that Jesus has commanded believers to "love one another," and that by this love "all will know that you are My disciples" (John 13:34–35). Yes, I also know that a Christian is to "esteem others better than himself" (Philippians 2:3). Yet I fail time and time again. Instead of being a Christian soldier for unity, I turn on a fellow soldier, carefully aim my weapon, and let loose my angry accumulation of acid ammunition.

I have often thought that the world can listen to us today and make this fair judgment, "See how they hate one another!"

James wisely analyzes the problem. "Where do wars and fights come from among you? Do they not come from your desires for pleasure that war in your members?" (James 4:1).

The writing team of Beeson and Hunsicker explain the passage like this. "What desires drive us to crush our brothers and sisters in Christ? For some the motivation is greed, ambition, or envy. For others it is the burning desire to be right in an ultimate, authoritative sense, the unbending determination to have the final word.

"Of course, we don't recognize these sins as our motives. We say we want purity and holiness in the church, more spiritual leadership, a return to biblical authority. We may even begin our fight with clean hands and hearts, but then the twin tempters Pride and Power rush to help us win. Before we realize it, we torch part of the body of Christ without much remorse."[5]

Two Women—Two Responses

It's so subtle. Of course, that's what we can expect from the Father of Lies, the Great Deceiver. Deborah had a fine voice. She had sung in the choir in the little church for years. She was accustomed to singing solos. She delighted in singing "for the Lord."

In time, she moved and began to attend a "megachurch." She tried out for the choir and made it. Because this was a large choir in a huge church the soloists were of superior quality. Deborah felt she had the "right" to be a soloist. She was not happy about being in the last row, week after week. She resented being passed over for special solos. She was miffed at not being included for a solo part in the Christmas production.

She did not keep her mouth shut. But did she go to the choir director? "No, it wouldn't do any good!" was her excuse. She did fume and fuss to any and all who would listen. "It's not fair! My voice is every bit as good as hers," she complained. "I can't stand the church politics!" She stirred up a lot of strife before she left the church.

Was she right? Maybe. Were there "church politics"? Possibly. Was her voice "as good as" the others? Perhaps so. Yes, she was a wounded "in action," but her response prevented any type of healing. Even today she will moan and groan about the church, the choir, the unfair treatment, until her griping clears the room of others who are tired of hearing it.

Contrast Deborah's response with that of another.

Mildred had been a legal secretary. She had married, raised a family, and was now widowed. She needed a job and applied at the church. She was hired as the head pastor's secretary. Because the church was large this was considered to be a position of some power, prestige, and authority.

Mildred was quiet, efficient, and dependable. Yes, she was older than the other secretaries on the staff. She was in her late fifties. A younger, ambitious woman on a lower rung of the church secretarial ladder coveted Mildred's job. She began to plant seeds with the "right" people. "Don't you think Mildred is a little slow? Of course, she *is* older. I don't see how she can possibly keep up with the load of work."

Mildred found out about the personal attacks. She kept silent. "My Father in heaven gave me the job and it will be mine until He wants me out," she confided to her sister. The verbal abuse behind her back continued. Mildred continued doing her job as she believed God had enabled her to do.

Like a slow-dripping faucet, the months of slander accomplished the desired result. Mildred was demoted to a position of assistant secretary in a different department. The younger woman had won. The coveted position as secretary to the head pastor was hers.

Mildred was hurt, but she respected the decision as coming from God himself. "I believe that God is sovereign and totally in control. Yes, it cuts like a knife. I don't know why I lost the job, but He does. I don't know why the pastor didn't defend me, but God does. The Lord has never let me down yet. He has provided an easier, less stressful position for me for His purposes. I will accept it and do my best. I will miss the higher salary, but God will provide. He always has and He always will. My verses are Philippians 4:19 and Philippians 4:11: 'And my God shall supply all your need according to His riches in glory by Christ Jesus.' 'Not that I speak in regard to need, for I have learned in whatever state I am, to be content.' "

If the Christian army were composed of Mildreds, the battlefield would be free of wounded! She is one beautiful lady who really "walks the talk!" Figure it out. When we get to heaven who gets the greater reward? The schemer or the saint?

Those precious women who are called of God to become pastors' wives could each write *The Big Book of Christian Hurts*. I have had the privilege of knowing several such Christian heroines through a period of many years. My admiration has skyrocketed as I have known the hurts within the Christian community that each has not only endured but triumphed over through the indwelling power of the Holy Spirit, applying the Word of God in their lives.

Sally

Sally is the pastor's wife of a small congregation. Her short, curly black hair is now tinged with what she refers to as "gray wisdom." In her soft sweet voice, she sadly recalls, "When we first started out I was young and inexperienced. People expected so much. They looked to me for wisdom and leadership I was not prepared to give. I didn't know how. I was in over my head. I made mistakes—a lot of mistakes. I admitted them then, and I admit them now. Instead of forgiving and encouraging me, the congregation crucified me with their razor-edged tongues.

"My poor husband! We were forced to leave the church, and all because of me and my mistakes. It was humiliating and degrading. My husband was gracious. I wasn't. I expected the older Christian women to be kind and supportive and helpful. Wrong.

"I never wanted to be a pastor's wife again. I wanted him to seek other employment. But he felt called of God to the ministry. That made me furious with him and disappointed with God. Of course, I was still very angry at the women who had made my life miserable.

"Yes, I had a lot of forgiving to do before God could use me effectively anywhere. I held on to my anger for years, and it poisoned every single relationship in every single church. I was so unhappy. I was on anger overload.

"I was desperate. Something had to change. I was in therapy and on pills. Nothing really helped. I was always on the verge of a nervous breakdown. Finally, in sheer desperation, I gave up. I pleaded with God to either take me or release me of the poison of my unforgiving spirit.

"Oh, how I wept! When I thought I was through, and had no tears left, I wept some more. It was such relief to let go of my anger. It took years for me to get to the point of wanting to forgive those wretched women.

"For me, forgiveness has been a long process. I have taken many baby steps of forgiveness in the past three years. Neither God nor my husband ever gave up on me. How I praise the Lord for such love, mercy, and patience!"

I asked Sally what she would like to say to other Christian women. She smiled and said, "Finally, I have some words of wisdom. If you are a woman in the congregation, and a young pastor's wife comes, I beg you in the name of Jesus, please uphold her in fervent prayer rather than gossiping. She needs the benefit of your prayers to help her grow through her youth and inexperience. For a pastor's wife or any other woman who has been singed with the torch of gossip, I plead with you: Don't hold on to your anger. Forgive, forgive, forgive, and then—forgive again. Otherwise you will be the one to suffer untold misery. Unforgiveness is too big a load to carry. Ephesians 4:32 has become my verse. I pray that God will make it real in my life: "Be kind to one another, tenderhearted, forgiving one another, just as God in Christ also forgave you."

Carol

Carol is the extremely talented but very humble and unassuming pastor's wife of a small congregation. Her husband has full-time outside employment in addition to the pastorate. It was in coming to know Carol as a master in the art of pottery that we first spoke of Christian hurts.

"In a tiny church like ours the women become close friends. I used to share everything. I was completely open and transparent. When a family leaves the church, it is very personal. I lose a friend I've loved. My children lose favorite friends and playmates.

"The hurts feel like betrayal. The first time we went through it, it came as such a shock. Of course we were close friends. My husband and I did whatever we could to minister to their needs. We spent hours in marriage counseling. Since there were financial problems, we brought food over, helped with laundry, that kind of thing. Two weeks later, they wrote a letter indicating this was not where God wanted them. They left the church. Now they are divorced. They didn't want to listen. They took the easy way out. They made up their own mind.

"It is frustrating. You want to give your heart. We are shepherds. We want to protect and to help. The prayer of my heart is that the Lord strengthen my heart and soften my husband's. He gets hard. Walls go up. He doesn't want to let people in anymore. But in order to have a shepherd's heart, you don't have the luxury of being offended and having thin skin. You must bear up.

"I'm at a place right now where I have one close friend, but I'm afraid to let her in too much because of what's happened in the past. I really appreciate her. But you know, as soon as someone says, 'I love you. We'd never leave the church,' that's the kiss of death. They'll be gone in three weeks. It's almost a joke!

"It's so interesting. Instead of following the principle of Scripture as stated in Matthew 18 and going directly to the person and discussing issues, people just leave. It's easier for them to leave than to address issues.

"I think the enemy uses hurts to incapacitate. Jesus was hurt. All the disciples left him. I think we're almost down to that. Jesus forgave Peter and all of them. We must take heart. We are going to be rejected, whether for Him or for us. We are also going to offend. We have got to learn to forgive and get past petty hurts."

I asked Carol, "How do you keep from caving in?" She responded, "Knowing that people will always let you down, you draw closer to the Lord and depend totally on Him. We cling to His Word. God always provides. If we keep our eyes on Jesus, we're not going to lose sight. If we look at the circumstances, down we go. Jesus is our only constant.

"I cling to several verses, and think about them all the time. 'And we know that all things work together for good to those who love God, to those who are the called according to his purpose' (Romans 8:28). Another favorite of mine is, 'You will keep him in perfect peace, whose mind is stayed on you' (Isaiah 26:3). If all we've been through can help someone else, it will have all been worthwhile. That makes me think of 2 Corinthians 1:4: '[God], who comforts us in all our tribulation, that we may be able to comfort those who are in any trouble, with the comfort with which we ourselves are comforted by God.' "

The wise words spoken by these women who have triumphed through many trials are gems of truth for all Christian women.

Steps to God-Confidence
When You Have Been Wronged

First, identify with Jesus. Scripture assures us that Jesus was "despised and rejected by men, a man of sorrows and acquainted with grief" (Isaiah 53:3). Jesus was humiliated: He "endured the cross, despising the shame" (Hebrews 12:2).

As you may have guessed, I believe in blatant honesty with the Lord. He already knows my heart, so there is no good reason to try to hide any thought or emotion from Him. The Lord is always gracious, forgiving—and He never, ever tells! The Lord is the only One you and I can talk to and have perfect assurance that our innermost thoughts and feelings are safe from the scrutiny of others.

I had a real struggle with becoming a Christian. I was raised in a Christian home and always went to church. I also went to a Christian school. I looked around. There was not one female role model I wanted to emulate. I didn't want to look like any of them, talk like any of them, or live my life like any of them. I was still in elementary school at the time.

Now I believe in heaven and hell. I didn't want to go to hell but I couldn't take being like "them." As I approached adolescence I came under conviction. I knew I was a sinner and needed forgiveness. I spent hours alone contemplating the deep thoughts of salvation—pro and con. As I was in the midst of decision-making, I came across two verses that transformed my life. Second Corinthians 10:12 tells us that "they, measuring themselves by themselves, and comparing themselves among themselves, are not wise." That's exactly what I was doing. I was looking around at other women and thinking, "Nope! I sure don't want to ever be like her!" That was wrong. What then? The true yardstick is found in Ephesians 4:13 ". . . the measure of the stature of the fullness Christ." Yes, for me, that was the missing link.

We are never to compare ourselves with others. We are to look only to Jesus Christ himself as our guide, our role model, our example.

That made perfect sense to me. I accepted the Lord Jesus as my own personal Savior.

Any woman who has ever looked to another woman for the "perfect role model" has been disappointed in some way. But as an old song goes, "There is no disappointment in Jesus, He is all that He promised to be!" In the Christian life honesty is the only policy! The Lord uses our honesty to lead us to the knowledge of himself. Jeremiah 29:13 assures us, "And you will seek Me and find Me, when you search for Me with all your heart."

Second, remember: God is who He says He is! God is sovereign. He really is in control of everything at all times! God is never ridden with anxiety or worried about anything. He does know what's best for us, but *we must trust*. Many times that is difficult, especially when all we want is something that seems so right for us—and another Christian let's us down.

Missy is very tall and thin, with a big smile and an infectious laugh. "My journey into deeper growth started just after I became fed up with living life my own way. I determined to live for God 'from this day forward.' I had been rebellious, and part of my disobedience had been dating a non-Christian and looking for fulfillment in a guy. So I decided to not even date. I wasn't even looking.

"I went to a Bible study—the first thing that happened was that I met this wonderful new guy. He was everything I think I ever wanted in a man. He was tall, handsome, and a strong leader. He knew what he wanted, he went after it, and got it. I always admired that.

"I was being mentored by a godly woman and was under her scrutiny. I believed I was doing everything right, so I became convinced that this guy was God's gift to me for marriage.

"He led me to believe that too, by things he would say. Such as, 'I'm just going to have to marry you,' and, 'I'd love to kiss you right now, but not until I know you're mine.' Of course I was thrilled by this.

"Then suddenly he started acting weird. For three days he didn't call. I couldn't believe what was going on. I couldn't understand it. I went back over my actions. *Have I done anything to cause this? What have I done?* I saw him at Bible study. He wasn't the same.

"Then he called. 'I need to talk to you.' I knew it was the end. I didn't know how to deal with it. I asked him to tell me over the phone. He said, 'I have to see you in person.'

"I went into our meeting thinking, 'Lord let me accept whatever comes from your hand. Lord, guard every word I say.'

"It was a short meeting. First he told me all the good things he thought about me. Then he said, 'But I don't love you the way I need to love a wife.' Everything in me screamed, *Why?* But I quenched my whys, accepting it from God's hand, while bawling in front of the guy. He said, 'Let's pray.' I was crying so hard I don't remember what he prayed. I prayed something like 'Thank you for the time we've had. Bring someone to complete him.'

"The real adventure with God began after this meeting. I was counseled to stay in the Bible study. I wondered, *How can I stay in the same room with him?* Proverbs 28:1 came to me: 'The wicked flee when no one pursues, but the righteous are bold as a lion.' I made it through the first night—just barely.

"We spoke, but it was so different, so strange.

"I had gone to church with him every week and sat with him. Now I was alone. I felt exposed, vulnerable. I arranged to sit with a friend, but we didn't connect. I sat by myself, tears streaming down my face the whole service.

"I kept thinking, 'This separation is just a trial. God will bring us back together.' No matter where I was, if a tall shadow appeared in the corner of my eye my heart would start to pound. I was certain it was him! I had such anxiety. Oh, how I wanted to run away, but was counseled, 'You can't jump out of the boat. You must go through the trial.'

"When he was near, the only way I kept my sanity was to cling to verses and to remember, 'He didn't do this. God did this!' Romans 11:33 assured me, 'Oh, the depth of the riches both of the wisdom and the knowledge of God! How unsearchable are His judgments and His ways past finding out!' I could not understand any of this. I had to trust God.

"Jeremiah 29:11 brought incredible comfort: ' "For I

know the plans I have for you," declares the Lord, "plans to prosper you and not to harm you, plans to give you hope and a future." '

"My desire to be with this man was very strong. For one solid year I prayed fervently every day for God to change his heart, to bring him back to me. God did not answer that prayer but worked in my heart. Finally, I was able to pray that God would take the desire for him away.

"My spiritual and emotional recovery took two years. He was not God's man for me. God gave him someone, and has given me the man He planned for me to have."

I asked Missy what she wanted to say to Christian women like herself. "You've got to remember to take the human factor out of it. God did it. You have to ask yourself what God wants you to learn through this. Psalm 31:14–15 is so great: 'But as for me, I trust in You, O Lord; I say, You are my God. My times are in Your hand.' Before the trial, I knew about God, now I know God. I've seen Him at work."

Third, thank the Lord for the trial that He has allowed. Trust Him to accomplish His purposes.

That is so terribly hard, when all we want is to be understood, vindicated, loved, appreciated, and accepted for who we are in Jesus—and—removed from the pain A.S.A.P.

Emily and Fred have been our friends for over two decades. Their love for the Lord radiates. Their zeal and passion for the ministry has been extraordinary as they have been severely wounded again and again. Just when I was certain a piercing blow would finish them off, they would come back rejoicing, stronger than ever. I just shake my head in never-ending amazement at how God gives them His love, His joy, and His forgiveness.

Since I usually speak with both of them, it seemed natural to conduct the interview in the same way. I first asked Emily what was the most difficult hurt from other Christians. She swiftly responded, "The hardest thing for me is to see the way other men treat my husband's style of leadership. Instead of respecting his integrity and his special giftedness, they always seem to search for flaws. It has sometimes really been character assassination. They want to destroy and discourage. The criticism is destructive rather than constructive.

"When this all began, I should have encouraged Fred and reaffirmed him. I know I have often added to his stress by not doing this as much as I could. I didn't because I was in a state of shock or denial. Christians can't be doing this! I couldn't accept that this was happening. Hearing it was so painful. I wanted to give help in the form of solutions, answers. But truly, there were no answers to give. Solutions to problems would not have solved anything. The persecution directed at my husband went beyond anything tangible.

"This form of intense abuse within the church leadership went on for several years. I kept thinking, 'God is going to take care of this!' "

I asked, "Why didn't you just bail out?" Fred's answer flashed back in an instant:

"I feel like being in the ministry is the greatest joy of my heart, even though it is the greatest pain. God has gifted me. His hand is in it. I can go back to the blessings and the confirmation. I know that the servant will not be greater than the master. I must be willing to suffer. What I didn't realize years ago is that it would be at the hands of believers. Those at the top, so to speak, give out the worst pain. But God uses those circumstances. He is able to meet my needs, to protect me. I know that if my heart is right toward Him, He'll move heaven and earth. Even through conflicts and warfare, I have to ask, 'How can I respond properly?' Nobody can take my joy away if it's grounded in Him and not my circumstances!

"When God has called you He will sustain you. We've seen it happen. When my response is right, I sense my own character growing, strengthening. I can go through things now I could never have handled in the past.

"There will always be attacks. I know that. If you leave

a church, the next place might be worse. The Lord went through cycles of trial and blessing. The desert was a trial. Then He was ministered to by angels—a great blessing. On earth He was accepted for a period of time, then experienced the terrible rejection that led to His crucifixion. Then came the great blessing of His resurrection and ascension. If He went through these cycles, why shouldn't we?"

For Fred and Emily, Psalm 37 has become their life memory passage. In quoting the psalm, they highlighted these words: "Do not fret because of evildoers [even if they are unwitting fellow Christians], nor be envious of the workers of iniquity. . . . Trust in the Lord, and do good; Dwell in the land, and feed on His faithfulness. Delight yourself also in the Lord, and He shall give you the desires of your heart. Commit your way to the Lord, trust also in Him, and He shall bring it to pass. . . . Rest in the Lord, and wait patiently for Him."

I asked for their words of wisdom for hurting Christians. They swiftly shared, "Here are four techniques to help you. They have helped us make it through time and time again:

1. *Thank the Lord for helping you die to self.* You don't have to defend yourself. When Christians attack and misunderstand, it causes us to look to Him. The Lord is doing us a favor.

2. *Thank the Lord for the things you are gaining from it.* You are getting an eternal perspective. Second Corinthians 4:17 assures us that "our light affliction, which is but for a moment, is working for us a far more exceeding and eternal weight of glory." No matter what we suffer, it is light in comparison to what Jesus suffered. Also remember, our time here on earth is like the snap of a finger when compared with eternity.

3. *Thank the Lord that you are one day closer to heaven.* That gives hope. As the old song goes,

"This world is not my home. I'm just passin' through. . . ."

4. *Thank the Lord for what He's given you*—a job, a family, the necessities of life. Too often we take little things for granted. We need to have a grateful attitude even in the midst of conflict.

Fourth, choose to forgive those who have wounded and wronged you.

It's kind of like touching an exposed nerve, isn't it? Forgiving—really forgiving—someone who has hurt you, when you are still convinced beyond the shadow of a doubt that you were right about whatever, is one of the most difficult things for any Christian woman to do.

C. S. Lewis understood this and said, "Everyone says forgiveness is a lovely idea until they have something to forgive."

Isn't that the truth? For one thing, to forgive—really forgive—someone requires of me that I humble myself. And for me, humble is h-a-r-d! Humble means I have to choose to let go of the hurt rather than wear it like some badge of honor. Humble is a little like putting a hat on a hurricane as I try to get my gusts of "righteous indignation" under control.

Only God can tenderize us into wanting to forgive. Frequently, a wounded Christian is all too ready, willing, and able to recite the precise details of past wrongs done by another in the body of Christ . . . years later! This steady dripping of acid from a treacherous tongue is utterly destructive. Think of each unforgiven wrong as a poison pellet that is injected into the bloodstream of the body of Christ. In time, the entire body feels the weakening effects of the bitter poison. Strength, joy, and vitality are dissipated as the poison takes over the body.

"Any doubt we might have about the serious damage Christian division brings to our personal relationship with Jesus is settled by the apostle John. In his epistle to the church, he writes: "We know that we have passed from death to life, because we love the brethren. He who does not love his brother abides in death" (1 John 3:14). Our salvation remains, but our daily experience of Christ's presence and power soon disappears. The more our love for other believers declines, the more Satan reigns."[6]

Intellectually, you and I know all that. Living it out practically is another matter altogether—as Jan knows so very well. Jan is worn and wounded.

Jan begins her story with a disclaimer, "Don't even try to guess who I am. You'll never know. My story is just one more sex scandal in the ministry. If it weren't my story, it would seem almost commonplace.

"Like many Christian married women, I thought it would never happen to me. My husband was the senior pastor in an expanding church. I was the devoted wife and mother of our growing family.

"Everything was good. Perhaps too good. I was always treated well by my husband. I must emphasize that. He never neglected me or the children. Sure he was busy and gone a lot, but that's true for a lot of men whose jobs mean extra hours and travel time.

"Yes, women were drawn to him because of his position and personality. We frequently joked about it. Women needed counseling and wanted it from him. I always believed that only women should counsel women, but he made himself available to help.

"In this case, the availability turned into something much more. She was an attractive woman in our church. She had a sad story . . . don't we all? He was counseling her regularly. She would call at our home for comfort. At first he was somewhat annoyed at the invasion of privacy, but after hearing her pathetic voice on the phone I even encouraged him. 'She needs you,' I remember saying. 'She sounds like she's falling apart. Maybe you'd better go to her.' Well, he went to her, and then went for her—mornings, afternoons, evenings.

Only, stupid me, I didn't know.

"After months of this, some people in the church ran into them in some obscure place out of town. The explanation was somewhat reasonable. 'We just happened to run into each other.' I was so naive and trusting.

"Later I discovered she was dropping little zingers. 'Poor man. His wife doesn't really understand him.' Or, 'She's so unavailable to meet his needs. She's always busy with the children. She has no time for him.' Another was, 'You know, his wife is so demanding!'

"At this point, their little affair had gone on for well over a year. Hearing the gossip made me suspicious, but I was still not convinced. What to do? This sounds so stupid, I'm ashamed to tell it, but I began going through his pockets, smelling his clothes, checking charges—looking for *something*. In my heart I wanted to find nothing, but I had this nagging doubt. I found some questionable things, but nothing concrete.

"In time, I saw a couple of exchanged glances between them at church that could have steamed up the windows. My heart began to ache. Still I said nothing except to one trusted friend outside the church.

"The gossip circulating about me increased. Words like 'mentally unbalanced' were thrown around. I confronted my husband. He pooh-poohed the whole thing and took me away for a 'second honeymoon.' I was somewhat comforted, but not completely.

"By this time, nearly two years had gone by. I had to know. I'd scrimped and saved enough money to hire a private detective. His report was complete with photos. I felt like my life had just ended. My rage at the long-term betrayal and my own stupidity was nearly uncontrollable. I confronted them both at one of their regular meeting places. My husband was aghast. I think the woman was actually relieved. Now that I knew, she figured she'd get her man.

"My nightmare was just beginning and continued

for over a year. The women in the church blamed me! They said I drove him to it. They wanted me to leave and him to stay! I was completely unprepared for that reaction. What little life I had left after the shock seemed to seep out of me. I barely had enough strength to love and care for our children.

"My husband did not want to leave me or the church. That intensified the problems between him and the other woman, and between him and me and the church. The events that followed are a blur.

"I spent hours with the Lord, alone, weeping, trying to understand, trying to sort out. Was it my fault? By now I wasn't sure. Why did my Lord and my God let it happen? Angry, poisoned thoughts consumed me. That led to severe depression. Oh, how I spent time in the Psalms of David. I probably would have committed suicide had it not been for the Word of God. I memorized Psalm 43. It became mine. I said it and thought about it during the day, and during the long, sleepless, dark nights: 'Vindicate me, O God, and plead my cause against an ungodly nation; oh, deliver me from the deceitful and unjust man! For thou are the God of my strength; why do you cast me off? Why do I go mourning because of the oppression of the enemy? Oh, send out your light and your truth! Let them lead me; let them bring me to your holy hill and to your tabernacle. Then I will go to the altar of God, to God my exceeding joy; and on the harp I will praise you, O God, my God. Why are you cast down, O my soul? And why are you disquieted within me? Hope in God; for I shall yet praise him, the help of my countenance and my God.'

"My husband eventually left me, left the church, and went away with the other woman. I left the church, of course. What didn't leave was the anger, the bitterness, the unforgiveness. I had such a spiritual struggle for the next few years. I needed to forgive my husband, the women in the church, and the other woman, and forgive myself for allowing myself to become poisoned and bitter. Second Corinthians 10:4–5 were key verses for me in this spiritual battle against unforgiveness: 'For the weapons of our warfare are not carnal but mighty in God for pulling down strongholds, casting down arguments and every high thing that exalts itself against the knowledge of God, bringing every thought into captivity to the obedience of Christ.'

"My unforgiving spirit was a towering stronghold that needed to crumble. It took a miracle of healing that only God could do. I would choose to forgive. Then it would all come back again. This verse was a tremendous help. I pleaded with God to bring my bitter and angry thoughts into captivity to the obedience of Christ. God faithfully answered again and again."

When I asked her what she would like to say to any woman facing any part of her story, she said, "You must forgive. You cannot endure the bitter bondage of an unforgiving spirit. Unforgiveness is a cruel taskmaster that destroys. It doesn't matter who is right and who is wrong. God's forgiveness heals and restores. Leave the results of your marriage, the other woman, and church politics to Jesus. Focus on God and on gaining His strength and forgiveness. Without this God-given forgiveness, there can be no hope."

Choosing to forgive fellow believers is the first step. Appropriating the power of Almighty God through His Word and persevering prayer is second. The healing of the mind and thought processes follows.

Charles Stanley has written a book entitled *Forgiveness*. In it he writes, "Forgiveness is a process that can be painful and at times seem unending. Whatever our pain, whatever our situation, we cannot afford to hold on to an unforgiving spirit another day. We must get involved with the process of forgiving others and find out what it means to be really free. If we will persevere and keep our eyes on the One who forgave us, it will be a liberating force like nothing else we have ever experienced."[7]

Fifth, ask the Lord to give you His love for other Christians.

This kind of love is definitely not a feeling! Because we Christians can be so very unlovely in word and in deed, this love can only come from God himself.

Sixth, M&M—*Memorize and meditate.*

The key verses in this chapter are crucial to dealing with Christian hurts.

Mildred: Philippians 4:19—"And my God shall supply all your need according to his riches in glory by Christ Jesus."

Philippians 4:11—"Not that I speak in regard to need, for I have learned in whatever state I am, to be content."

Sally: Ephesians 4:32—"And be kind to one another, tenderhearted, forgiving one another, just as God in Christ also forgave you."

Carol: Romans 8:28—"And we know that all things work together for good to those who love God, to those who are the called according to his purpose."

Isaiah 26:3—"You will keep him in perfect peace, whose mind is stayed on you."

Carol: 2 Corinthians 1:4—"[God], who comforts us in all our tribulation, that we may be able to comfort those who are in any trouble, with the comfort with which we ourselves are comforted by God."

Pat: Jeremiah 29:13—"And you will seek me and find me, when you search for me with all your heart."

Missy: Proverbs 28:1—"The wicked flee when no one pursues; but the righteous are bold as a lion."

Romans 11:33—"Oh, the depth of the riches both of the wisdom and knowledge of God! How unsearchable are his judgments and his ways past finding out!"

Jeremiah 29:11—" 'For I know the plans I have for you,' declares the Lord, 'plans to prosper you and not to harm you, plans to give you a hope and a future.' "

Psalm 31:14–15—"But as for me, I trust in you, O Lord; I say, 'You are my God.' My times are in your hand."

Fred & Emily: Psalm 37—"Do not fret because of evildoers, nor be envious of the workers of iniquity. . . . Trust in the Lord, and do good; dwell in the land, and feed on his faithfulness. Delight yourself also in the Lord; and he shall give you the desires of your heart. Commit your way to the Lord, Trust also in him, and he shall bring it to pass. . . . Rest in the Lord, and wait patiently for him."

2 Corinthians 4:17—"For our light affliction, which is but for a moment, is working for us a far more exceeding and eternal weight of glory."

Jan: Psalm 43—"Vindicate me, O God, and plead my cause against an ungodly nation; Oh, deliver me from the deceitful and unjust man! For you are the God of my strength."

2 Corinthians 10:4—"For the weapons of our warfare are not carnal, but mighty in God for pulling down strongholds, casting down arguments and every high thing that exalts itself against the knowledge of God, bringing every thought into captivity to the obedience of Christ."

Reflections

1. What is your biggest problem with other Christians?

_____

_____

_____

2. Have you ever been wounded by a fellow Christian? Ex-

plain the most difficult situation and include your response.

_____

_____

_____

_____

_____

_____

3. In your opinion, how do the Christians you know respond to hurts within the body of Christ? Please be specific.

_____

_____

_____

_____

_____

_____

_____

4. When do you find it easiest to love other Christians?

_____

_____

_____

5. When is it the most difficult for you to love other Christians? How do you handle these situations?

_____

_____

_____

_____

_____

6. How would you describe the body of Christ as you have come to know it?

_____

_____

_____

_____

_____

_____

_____

7. Of the stories shared in this chapter, which affected you most deeply?

_____

_____

_____

8. Have you experienced the bondage of an unforgiving spirit as well as the freedom of forgiveness?

_____

_____

9. Please write a personal comment on each of the six steps to God-confidence in the area of Christian hurts.

_____

_____

_____

_____

_____

_____

_____

10. Select one or more verse for your own personal "M&M." Write them down.

_____

_____

_____

_____

_____

_____

_____

_____

_____

_____

11. After you have committed the first verse to memory, and are beginning to think about it during the day, explain how God is using it in your life.

_____

_____

_____

_____

Myth Ten

*Dearest Heavenly Father, just when I think I've learned so much about who you are and what you can do in my life–**BAM**! A crisis comes crashing into my fragile world, and my anxiety level skyrockets. I'm so disappointed. I thought I'd be further ahead by now with all you've taught me. Am I just a really slow learner, or what? You know my heart. I want to trust you at all times, and have the peace that passes understanding, but I am not making it.*

I know there will be loads of crises and tough times all through life. I can't handle any of them, but I know you can. Please teach me how to trust you moment by moment, and have your confidence in every situation at all times. I love you, Father. Thank you for never giving up on me! Thank you for your eternal love, mercy, patience, and compassion.

"I Can't Trust God When I'm in a Crisis."

IF I WERE A GOD-CONFIDENT WOMAN 100 percent of the time, I would always see "light" at the end of the tunnel! That would mean I was focusing on the Lord, and trusting Him for all things, in all situations, at all times! How I wish that were so!

In Chinese calligraphy, the words *dangerous opportunity* are joined together to make the word *crisis*. I fully understand the "danger"—it's all those things that I'm afraid might happen. During a crisis, those "but what if" thoughts are racing around my mind nonstop like mice on a treadmill. It's the "opportunity" I fail to see and tend to question God about.

If it weren't so sad, my reaction in a crisis would be amusing. When the crisis hits, I panic. I am aghast at the inconvenience. I question God. "God, where are you?" If you're in control, why did you let this happen to me?"

Then I give God subtle suggestions. "Please—get me out of this fast!"

Then I wait. Nothing. The crisis intensifies. I pray. The crisis persists. I pray harder for it to be over. Nothing. The crisis complications increase. Now it's hopeless.

At long last, I come to the end of myself. I give up my various manipulations with God. I give up the tantrum. I give up the self-pity. I even give up giving God all my great suggestions.

I become quiet before Him and begin to pray for His will, not mine. "Teach me to do your will. Honor yourself in this situation. Use me to bring you honor and glory. I will trust you to be faithful and to see me through this."

As soon as I give up all control and attempt at manipulating God and choose to let go and simply trust and obey, peace replaces panic.

In time, the particular crisis passes. Then I am the first one to tell everyone: "God was so faithful. Just listen to this. . . ." "You won't believe what God did!" "It was so hopeless. Then God . . ." "Let me share this fantastic verse. God used it in my life when . . ." "I had the most marvelous answer to prayer."

Strange, isn't it! We *know* God is faithful. We *know* He is worthy of our trust. We *know* He will see us through. Why do we still persist in a panic pattern when approaching a crisis? Because we are weak and frail human beings!

I know I'm weak, but I also know that my great God is strong. I know He won't give up on me, and that His "strength is made perfect in weakness" (2 Corinthians 12:9). That's what I call great encouragement!

I am also so thankful that He loves me unconditionally . . . in spite of my foolishness, my lack of trust, my doubts, my anxieties, my tantrums, my manipulations and endless strivings. On the back page of my Bible I have taped some wonderful words that were in our church bulletin one Sunday. No source was given. I am certain it will be of as much comfort and encouragement to you as it has been to me.

He Loved Me When

He loved me when my heart forgot.
His love for me was all I sought.
He loved me when my foolish dreams
Filled all my thoughts with worldly things.
He loved me when I walked away.
Down paths where none should ever stray.
He loved me when no other could—
No one loved me when my faith was low
And doubts assailed my troubled soul.
He loved me through those darkest nights,
Until my soul found heavenly light.

He loved when I felt alone,
No friends around and far from home.
He loved when no other could—
No one could love me more.
He loved me long before I knew
He came to earth for me and you.
He loved me so that others know
He is the source of love I show.
He loves me now for this I know,
His love will last when others go.
He loves me like no other could—
No one could love me more.
No one could love me more.

What a glorious reason for God-confidence—the attitude of heart and mind that calmly, confidently believes that God is in control of all things everywhere at all times, and so we are able to trust Him without reservation.

Just when you and I are slowly, steadily climbing toward increasing God-confidence, a crisis is bound to come. We will look down and see *nothing*! Then the roller-coaster ride begins. Only increasing God-confidence can help us to level the anxiety at times like these.

Let's take another look at each of the "self-esteem" destroyers in a crisis situation and review the Steps to God-confidence that will make the difference in crisis management.

CRISIS—Body Image

Madame Jeanne Marie Guyon (Gay-YON) was one of the most profoundly spiritual Christian writers of all time.

In 1663, her family moved to Paris, a pleasure-mad city under the reign of Louis XIV. As Jeanne matured, she grew into the tall beauty for which she was renowned. Jeanne's vanity and pride increased. Her beauty, intellect, and brilliant powers of conversation made her a favorite of Paris society. At the age of sixteen, her father arranged her marriage to M. Guyon, a thirty-eight-year-old man of great wealth and prominence.

Disillusionment set in for Jeanne like penetrating fog. God used this to turn her to himself. She began to spend less time in front of the mirror and more time looking to the Lord. She received definite assurance of salvation through faith in Christ when she was twenty years old.

After this experience, she exulted: "Nothing was more easy to me now than to practice prayer. Hours passed away like moments. . . . This love of God occupied my heart so constantly and strongly . . . nothing else seemed worth attention. I bade farewell forever to the amusements and pleasures that are so much prized and esteemed by the world. They now appear to me dull and insipid—so much so, that I wondered how I ever could have enjoyed them."[1]

When she was twenty-two years of age, she was stricken with a virulent case of smallpox. To a large extent her beauty was destroyed.

Everyone thought she would be inconsolable. But she wrote, "As I lay in my bed, suffering the total deprivation of that which had been a snare to my pride, I experienced a joy unspeakable. I praised God with profound silence. . . . When I was so far recovered as to be able to sit up in my bed, I ordered a mirror to be brought, and indulged my curiosity so far as to view myself in it. I was no longer what I was once. It was then I saw my heavenly Father had not been unfaithful in His work, but had ordered the sacrifice in all reality."[2]

The remainder of Madame Guyon's life was characterized by great simplicity and power. She left behind her about sixty volumes of writings. In this poem, written while a prisoner in the dreaded dungeon of Bastille, she expresses the depth of her Christian experience:

> To me remains nor place nor time;
> My country is in every clime;
> I can be calm and free from care
> On any shore since God is there.[3]

Very few have such great beauty or experience the dramatic loss of it as did Madame Guyon. Yet her "crisis management" is available to us regardless of the body-image crisis we may experience.

Body-Image Crisis Steps to God-Confidence

1. Ask Him to give you the wisdom to be your best. He cares. Matthew 10:30 tells us that even the hairs on our head are numbered.

2. Ask Him to give you appropriate goals for each area of appearance that concerns you.

3. Trust Him to do good things for you and with you.

4. Ask Him to make you content with who you are and how you are.

5. Ask Him to encourage you regarding your appearance.

6. Ask Him to deliver you from self-consciousness and self-absorption and to deliver you from comparisons.

7. Praise Him for what He has done, is doing, and will continue to do in your life.

8. Remember: It's OK to get discouraged. In each area of God-confidence, Satan will attempt to demean and repudiate your growth.

CRISIS—Health

Catherine Marshall was only twenty-three when she and her pastor husband, Peter, moved to Washington D.C., where he became pastor of the New York Avenue Presbyterian Church. Very quickly her husband's reputation as a deeply committed man of God grew. Congressmen, senators, and people from all walks of life attended the worship services.

At the peak of their ministry, Catherine was diagnosed with tuberculosis. The only treatment at the time was total rest. Doctors assured her she would be well in three to four months, but two years later her situation remained unchanged.

She fought feelings of depression as she watched her son and husband living a life separate from the one she was forced to maintain. Her journal became a spiritual solace where she recorded her talks with God and the hope He faithfully provided.

One night while staying at her parents' house, she was awakened with a sense of God's closeness. "I knew that Jesus was smiling at me tenderly, lovingly. . . . His attitude seemed to say, 'Relax! There's not a thing wrong here that I can't take care of.'

"The unforgettable truth of David's Psalm 23 came alive in my experience. This was a period of equipping, of spiritual preparation, for a tumultuous life of changes—of great, high moments, followed by plunging low points."

X-rays taken a short time later revealed a marked improvement. Within six months, the doctors pronounced her completely well. Catherine could write, "From the vantage point of the years, I can see now that my being forced to lie down in the green pastures beside very still waters—the isolation of our bedroom—was a time of training. Day by day God was the teacher and I the pupil. I would need Him every day for the rest of my life and throughout eternity."

A short time later when news of Peter's sudden death came, God provided the hope she needed: " 'Surely goodness and mercy shall follow [you] all the days of [your] life,' was His personal pledge to me and to a son who would now sorely miss his father."

Realizing she now had a much greater responsibility and purpose, Catherine went on to become a noted Christian author and speaker. At the end of her life she was able to say, "God has met me at every turn. It is the assurance that if He would deal so lovingly with someone like me, then you too can meet Him in a person-to-person encounter, feel His love for you, and know that He is the answer to every cry of your heart."[4]

The perils of ill health and disability surround each of us. Many of us walk through dark valleys as we watch the pain and struggle of a loved one.

Health-Crisis Steps to God-Confidence

1. Be completely honest with God. For each person who is triumphing in the arena of health problems, the first step toward a victorious attitude is honesty with God. And this is just as important with the routine concerns of bronchitis, bladder infections, PMS, as it is with life-threatening diseases.

2. Acknowledge that God is sovereign. He rules in every circumstance of life, including every cold, cough, ache, and pain. He is completely in control. He has allowed this infirmity for His purposes.

3. God is able to heal. Stay open to healing, even as you learn to go on with God in your illness.

4. God does not always choose to heal. Ask Him to strengthen you in Christ, so that His purposes for you may be accomplished.

5. Choose to trust that the Lord is doing what's best for each of us with eternity in view.

6. Out of our admitted weakness—physical, mental, emotional, and spiritual—can come His marvelous strength. Our God "has chosen the weak things of the world to put to shame the things which are mighty" (1 Corinthians 1:27). Our weakness is no hindrance to Him, but rather enables His strength to flow.

7. Ask God for wisdom in how best to use limited energy resources. So often, the "good" is the enemy of the "best." When you ask the Lord to guide your energy choices, He will. With God in charge, it is truly amazing how much He can accomplish through us—even with all our limitations!

CRISIS—Accomplishments

Of all the unimaginable things that I could ever become, principal of a school was the lowest on my list. It was a definite "never ever!" Once God taught me how to teach, I loved it. I knew that the classroom was where the fun was. Being a principal seemed quite dreadful. I had worked with many different administrators. Each seemed too busy, too stressed, too tired, too distracted, and spent their time doing too many no-fun things. I was adamant. That was the worst job of all in education, and I would never have it. One incredibly long and boring session of an administration class in graduate school convinced me: *Administration is not an option.* I switched my major immediately to something less loathsome and went on to my master's.

But because of what God taught me in disciplinary skills, my school district was encouraging me to go into administration.

Years went by. The children came, and so did working part time as a preschool director and as the director of a reading lab. That was plenty close enough to administration for my taste. Even as the children got older, I was content with my schedule.

"God works in mysterious ways." How true! One bright, sunny California afternoon, I was happily tutoring in the reading lab. The cheery voice on the intercom told me that a board member was on the phone. I vaguely wondered what he wanted. He got right to the point. Our administrator was in the hospital, and would be out for a while. He asked, "Would you like to take over the job while she's gone?" I answered quickly and succinctly, "No!" He put it another way. "Will you take the job while she's gone?" I laughed, and said, "OK." After all, how long could it be?

Well, so far it's been seven of the most wonderful years of my life! He has given me the greatest staff imaginable this side of heaven, the most supportive board of directors, cooperative parents, and the best children. Are there problems? What do *you* think? There are enough to keep us on our knees so that we never forget the Source of our hope, joy, and strength!

By the time I had refused the job offer three times, the Lord had softened my heart and given me His attitude. When I said *yes* I was certain that it was God's will for me, but I did not sleep one single second that night. All of the "buts," the "what ifs," the "I can'ts," the "I don't know hows" were accompanied by high mountains of anxiety.

In the early morning, God brought to my mind the wonderful words from Zechariah 4:6–7: " 'Not by might nor by power, but by My Spirit,' says the Lord of hosts. 'Who are you, O great mountain? Before Zerubbabel you shall become a plain!' " Next to that verse, I wrote the date, as I always do when the Lord gives a particular passage for a special crisis situation.

Because I know that God has called me to do this job for this moment in time, I also know that He has assumed the responsibility for equipping me with what I need to do the job "heartily, as to the Lord" (Colossians 3:23). The Lord has taken each high mountain peak of a problem and made it into a plain each time I keep my focus on Him and choose to trust and obey!

God has been so patient encouraging me to focus on Him, the problem-solver, rather than the problem. I'll sing over and over, "Great Is Thy Faithfulness!"

Accomplishment— Crisis Steps to God-Confidence

1. Share with the Lord your frustration, resentment, and anger in whatever areas of achievement that are bothering you.

2. Ask Him to either deliver you from the desire to achieve, to succeed, to excel, or to teach you how to do it.

3. Realize that God chooses to humble us of "self-esteem" so that we will learn to trust Him. Then He can

use you for the purposes He intends.

4. Never forget "when I am weak, then I am strong" through His power and strength (2 Corinthians 12:10). You and I will be able to do what God intends. Those high mountains of things that seem impossible to overcome really do become opportunities for God to demonstrate His overcoming power.

5. Ask the Lord to deliver you from impossible human expectations and from the curse of "comparisonitis." You are totally unique and different from anyone who has ever lived. There will never again be anyone just like you, and no one but you can do what God intends for you to do.

6. Trust the Lord to make changes in your attitude and also your performance.

7. Focus on applying Colossians 3:23 on a moment-by-moment basis. "Whatever [and that means everything from cleaning a toilet to running a business] you do, do it heartily, as to the Lord and not to men."

CRISIS—Things

For the past several years, life has been hard for Nell. Certainly nothing like the life she envisioned for herself when she married the handsome Air Force man. "I knew the Lord when I got married, but I had no teaching about 'being unequally yoked.' I fell in love with a non-believer and married him.

"He was assigned to the Philippines for four months. When he came back, he started saying things like, 'What if we get a divorce?' I was stunned. For me there was no such thing as divorce. Marriage was 'till death us do part.' Single parent was not in my vocabulary.

"There was another woman in the Philippines. They exchanged letters. Several months later, he filed for divorce. I was in a state of continual shock. Our daughter was two years old. Then I found out I was pregnant! I didn't want a divorce—ever! I even wrote to the other woman and told her about the pregnancy. My husband found out and was furious. When I was six months pregnant, he asked me to move out.

"This was particularly difficult because I had to have bedrest. My husband gave me some money, but I began to learn how to scrimp in a way I never thought I could.

"I couldn't afford an attorney. He had one. I said I didn't want the divorce. It didn't matter. He was given the divorce when the new baby was only two months old. There I was, alone with two small kids.

"Then I really began to learn about handling money in a brand-new way. My ex-husband was not paying what he should. I learned to feed the three of us on $40 a week. I ate less than my children. I sold everything I could sell and moved into a tiny one-bedroom apartment. Even though we were in Texas in the summer, I learned how to survive without using the air conditioner. The phone was used very little. Yet the Lord took care of us, and my health was good. Selling the stuff didn't bother me. I knew God was leading.

"But the future loomed ahead. How was I going to provide for my children? My older daughter had been premature. The Lord gave me a heart for taking care of 'preemies.' But how could I work, go to school, take care of my tiny children, pay for school and necessities? It was all too much.

"In complete exhaustion and weariness, I gave it to the Lord. I just didn't know how to do all this and financially survive. Again and again I just gave it back to the Lord.

"I started applying to colleges. I applied for loans and grants—for anything and everything possible. I didn't hear one word. I had a tiny income from being in the Air Force that I was hanging on to for security. I was scared to let it go and really have nothing.

"It was a Monday night. I said, 'Okay, Lord. I'm going to totally trust you.' I let go of the Air Force income by giving notice. I really believed God wanted me to be a nurse with preemies.

"After I let go completely, and decided to trust God, He

opened the doors. The loans and the grants came through.

"Yes, it has been a struggle. Every day, I'm still trying to survive, but God has provided all this time. I still have bad days—like today. I thought I was going to get a check today. There wasn't one because of the late paperwork. There won't be a check for 29 days. I was in tears. I cried to the Lord, 'I don't have food money. I have bills. What am I going to do, Lord?' I panicked for about fifteen minutes. 'I guess I'll have to borrow, and then pay it back at the end of the month.'

"God has provided people, His people, whom I can borrow from until I can pay them back. I have become humble. I have learned to swallow my pride. I have learned to talk to the Lord just like I'm talking to you."

I asked Nell what she would like to say to single moms in similar situations. "Romans 8:28 is so familiar, but it's my verse: 'And we know that all things work together for good to those who love God, to those who are the called according to His purpose.' God won't give you more than you can handle. You have to trust Him. That doesn't mean you don't work hard, but you trust the Lord about every single thing. Sometimes you have to be patient and not panic when the Lord does not come through until the last moment. Remember that He is your Provider. He is not going to let things happen to you that you can't handle.

"Somewhere I got the idea for a *Blessing Box.* I don't know where. You take an oatmeal carton, cover it with pretty wrapping paper, and cut an opening in the top. Then, whenever the Lord gives a blessing or answers a prayer, you write it on a piece of paper and slip it inside the box. On Thanksgiving, you open the box, take each of the slips of paper out and read them. Even in my hardest year the Blessing Box was full of blessings and answered prayer.

"I just want to say it again. Trust. Don't give up. I pray someone can benefit by knowing about how God is taking care of me and my girls."

Financial crises are all too familiar today regardless of

the income level. God does not change. He is the same Provider that He was all through the Bible and has been all through history. Only the names, faces, and particulars change. He will be faithful in His provision to His own. Nell found out what her responsibility was—to trust. It is the same for you and for me. We must choose to trust our Jehovah-Jireh.

"Things"—Crisis Steps to God-Confidence

1. Pour out the longings of your heart to God. Of course, God already knows, but we need to be honest with Him and with ourselves in order to pinpoint exactly what the "self-esteem" destroyer is. When God has our attention in an honest, forthright way, He begins to build God-confidence in His child.

2. Remember that our archenemy, Satan, wants us to be enslaved by the "things" of this world. There is a certain false hope of contentment in always pursuing but never quite attaining, which convinces us that we would be content *if* we "just had such and such!" Alas! We know this is false, yet we get trapped—again and again!

3. Ask the Lord to make you content with what He's already given!

4. "Seek first the kingdom of God and His righteousness, and all these things will be added to you" (Matthew 6:33).

5. Get serious in prayer with the Lord about freedom from debt and from wanting "stuff!" *Pray about everything!*

6. Rejoice and give thanks to God for what He is teaching you in this crucial area of life.

CRISIS—Time Management

Nothing can raise my blood pressure faster than a time-management catastrophe, especially when I think I've done everything right! I've planned properly, and allowed sufficient time. The problem is that I never plan for the *unexpected* that comes and pulverizes my time management to pieces. How stupid of me! The unexpected is the one thing that is sure to happen when my time is squeezed like the corset of a Southern Belle!

The unexpected always comes when we can't squeeze in any more time. But the unexpected cannot be ignored. It can be friends or relatives from out of town, dropping in unannounced for a week or so—expecting time, energy, and cash, all three of which are in short supply at the precise moment they enter the scene. Or the unexpected can be a sudden illness of a friend or family member who requires a lot of time. It can be a series of breakdowns around the house of things that are essential to the sane running of the household.

The unexpected can be a series of "have-to's" that didn't show up on the calendar for whatever reason. "I didn't know about. . . !" "You never told me I had to. . . !" Now here they all come, swift and steady, ready to trample what life is left in us!

The unexpected always happens. And there is *no way out*, humanly speaking. At times like this, I think of the title of an old musical, "Stop the World! I Want to Get Off!" That's what I'd like but that is not possible. . . .

Time-Management— Crisis Steps to God-Confidence:

1. Begin each day focusing on the Lord.

2. Realize that God never asks, expects, or wants us to "do it all"!

3. Realize that Jesus, our ultimate role model, never rushed around. And He often got away from people to spend time alone, in blissful solitude with His heavenly Father.

4. Ask the Lord to give you the wisdom to know when to say *yes* and the courage to say *no*.

5. Ask God to give you the wisdom to know how to or-

ganize and manage efficiently and effectively the time He has given to you. It is in His power to train us to use it in the best possible way to accomplish what He desires.

6. Learn to wait on the Lord!

CRISIS—Men

There it was, on the top of the stack of mail: *summons to jury duty.* My heart sank. When I reported in, I realized I had not yet asked the Lord to give me His attitude. My body language was clear: *This lady does not want to be here.* The room was packed with people with similar attitudes. Role call sounded like the barking of angry dogs.

As soon as possible I headed for the snack bar for a cup of coffee. I sat down by myself at a table and tried to spread out and relax. Then an attractive brunette sat down next to me. *What nerve!* I looked up just long enough to realize that she had actually dressed for the occasion. I looked like a refugee from a leftover grab bag. She was coordinated and immaculately groomed, every hair in place.

Oh great! Now I felt ugly on top of my bad attitude. I was silently castigating myself for my slovenly attire when a voice on the intercom said something that needed interpretation. The two of us began talking, trying to decipher the code.

I have to laugh in retrospect. God has such a glorious sense of humor. I discovered shortly that Shari was a very special Christian woman. The next few hours sped by as she opened her heart and shared her story. She has given me permission to share it with you:

Shari had been married nearly twenty years when her police officer husband was present at the killing of a suspect by his rookie partner. Shari's husband, who was a Christian, did not believe the killing was justified.

The events in the department surrounding the incident precipitated Post Traumatic Stress Syndrome in Shari's husband. The department required him to see their psychologist.

"The meetings included prying into all the personal aspects of our marriage and family life. After several such sessions, the psychologist came to the conclusion that a lot of my husband's stress was related more to our marriage than to the shooting.

"At home his behavior changed. He became dissatisfied, would find fault with little things. I was surprised. I didn't understand. We'd had a normal marriage, though not perfect.

"After four months of weekly visits, the dissatisfaction accelerated. He began to say things like, 'I can understand why a man would have an affair.'

"My husband was always very open. He began meeting the psychologist for breakfast once a week or so 'off the record.' I thought this was strange, and not a professional way of handling the situation.

"The department was paying for all this, of course. Then I was called in. The psychologist was a very attractive woman, and, as I found out, was recently separated from her husband! In the course of the conversation she told me what she had told my husband, that she did not feel the stress was so much related to the shooting as it was to our marriage. She also mentioned my 'biblical approach' to things, indicating that such an approach contributed to stress in the marriage. She recommended that we separate for the sake of my husband's stress.

"At her recommendation, my husband spent a month in a psychiatric hospital. She was no longer his therapist. To my knowledge she did not visit him. She called us, however, to see how we were doing, and seemed to take a real interest in the family. I even sent her a thank-you note.

"When he got out of the hospital, my husband did not want to come home. He moved in with friends. I called the psychologist and told her he'd moved out. She asked me to come in and bring the girls so she could explain what was going on. She told our daughters that their dad needed his space.

"When I asked why she couldn't counsel my husband

to keep his marriage intact she said she couldn't do that. I stormed out. The rest is a blur. I was in shock. I found out my husband continued to see the psychologist.

"I asked a godly man in our church, someone my husband respected, to counsel him. My husband refused the counsel, saying, 'I should have divorced her ten years ago!' He called me and said, 'Don't send me anyone else from the church.' Then he filed for divorce.

"I was devastated. There were times I just couldn't think. I'd never experienced anything like it before. I counseled with someone in the church who reminded me of 1 Thessalonians 5:18: 'In everything give thanks; for this is the will of God in Christ Jesus for you.' He suggested I thank God.

"I went home, walked into our study, and got down on my knees in front of a chair. It was difficult, but in thanking Him for the valley I was walking through, a peace flooded my soul. All the why's were removed. I wasn't wringing my hands anymore. I was not in total despair. I accepted that God had allowed this for a reason and a purpose. In thanking Him, I acknowledged His control.

"From that moment on, I stopped manipulating, trying to make things happen. I let go of my ideas and just prayed that He would work it out in the way He wanted. I made signs and put them around the house to remind me: 'Let go of your ideas, and let God. . . .'

"At the end of seven weeks, I wrote a letter to my husband totally releasing him from our marriage. I did not write it expecting him to come home. I wrote it for my peace of mind. I needed to get on with my life. The letter was not vindictive, not bitter, not controlling, not a putdown. I wanted it to be God speaking through me to my husband.

"When I knew the Lord was leading, I took the letter and put it in his mailbox. My husband called. He was very angry. 'Why would you write such a stupid letter? What do you mean—releasing me?' Then he hung up.

"Three days went by and he called asking to borrow my

car. That night he called again saying he needed to talk to me. He came over and told me he wanted to come home.

"He did come home, and we went to see our pastor. We renewed our marriage vows and are starting over again.

"You don't know until you've experienced it—but releasing my husband unconditionally was the real test of my Christianity.

Men—Crisis Steps to God-Confidence

1. Confess your anger, frustration, or helplessness in dealing with the men who mean so much in your life.

2. Face the fact that we women, particularly in the area of men, tend to get our focus off God, and choose to rely on our own resources—physical, mental, and emotional—to meet our perceived needs. Remember that by losing the God-focus, men then take the place of importance that only God should have, becoming idols in our lives.

3. Be aware that it is only when we "give up" and are broken and in a position where all the manipulations of our feminine wiles have failed that God can begin to do a wonderful work in our relationships with men.

4. Believe that God knows what (and who) is best for you, and that He cares more about your joy, contentment, and fulfillment than you do.

5. Remember that God can change lives in His way, in His time, and for His purposes. Remember too, that in any "change-over" God will include us!

6. Trust God to do wonderful things for you in your relationship with men, but only when you obediently seek Him first. God does give "beauty for ashes" and "the oil of joy for mourning" (Isaiah 61:3) in relationships with men. Forgiveness is crucial!

7. Look for changes and thank God; remember that your attitude and behavior need changing first. Then God, by the transforming power of His Holy Spirit, will be able to do incredible things in your relationships with men.

CRISIS—Christian Hurts

I crawled into the house, dead tired, hoping for a little rest before going back to school in the evening for our Open House.

Out of habit, I listened to the recorded messages on the answering machine. Only the one from a pastor in our church caught my attention. He was not someone who I spoke to on a regular basis. Years ago, I had tutored his older daughter in reading, and had minimal contact with the family since.

It was the serious tone of his voice that grabbed me. I knew he wasn't calling to thank me for twenty years of faithful service at the church working with children. But what could it possibly be? Naturally, I was curious. I dialed the number. The line was busy. I tried a couple more times. Still busy. By now it was time to leave for school.

The next morning I returned his call at my first opportunity. He was in a meeting. Then I was in a meeting when he called back. When we made a connection a little later, I first chatted breezily, asking about the family. My female intuition was right on. This was not a happy-go-lucky-you-are-loved-and-appreciated-and-we-just-wanted-you-to-know kind of call. Quite to the contrary. He was serious, and anxious to get to the point. I can still hear his wounding words: "You have been accused of something."

I was aghast! My heart began racing, my pulse pounding in my ears. I had no idea what he was talking about. I fought for composure. By his tone of voice, it had to be something awful! I can't recall exactly what I said, but I started praying, asking the Lord to give me His calm, His strength, His kindness, His graciousness, His wisdom. "Who is my accuser?" I finally asked.

He responded, "You don't know him."

That left me absolutely confounded. I wanted to get it settled, and asked if we could do it over the phone. "No! Your accuser must face you." He made me feel guilty of doing something despicable, but what? I had to know as soon as possible. I had an hour free without appointments. He said he would come to my office.

I called my husband. He was out of the office. I began walking around the campus, praying pieces from the Psalms—18, 46, 91:

> I will love thee O Lord, my strength. The Lord is my rock, and my fortress, and my deliverer; my God, my strength, in whom I will trust; my buckler, and the horn of my salvation, and my high tower. . . . God is [my] refuge and strength, a very present help in trouble. . . . He is my refuge and my fortress: my God; in Him will I trust. Surely He shall deliver thee from the snare of the fowler, and from the noisome pestilence. He shall cover thee with his feathers, and under His wings shalt thou trust: His truth shall be thy shield and buckler. Thou shalt not be afraid for the terror by night; nor for the arrow that flieth by day; nor for the pestilence that walketh in darkness; nor for the destruction that wasteth at noonday. . . . For He shall give His angels charge over thee, to keep thee in all thy ways. (KJV)

Over and over again I repeated these words. I had to fill my mind with Him, not with my fear and apprehension. My steps led to the library. My prayer partner and school librarian, Trudi, was alone. "Thank you, Lord." I shared with her and began to cry. "I know how cruel Christians can be. Please pray for me." She held my hands and prayed until the secretary came and told me that the two men I was expecting were in the office.

Fortified by the power of God's Word and prayer, I welcomed them to the school and ushered them into my office. We sat down. The pastor was curt. His question to the other man is indelibly printed in my mind. "Is she the woman?"

The younger man had been giving me searching glances. He answered without hesitation, "No!" I was somewhat relieved, but still wondering, still curious. The pastor was reticent to give any information. I gleaned that something had happened in the church parking lot late on Sunday night, and a woman who looked like me was involved. I made a feeble attempt at small talk. Apparently the younger man knew who I was from my work at church. Then I suggested we pray. The pastor prayed. They left. That was it.

I was still in shock. When my husband returned to the office, he called. Then the tears flowed freely. Although I could understand the need to discover "who did it," I could not comprehend the reason for the severity and callousness of the approach.

My husband spoke with the pastor, letting him know that his wife was "traumatized." The pastor believed he'd handled the matter correctly. My husband asked, "What was going on in the parking lot?" He was told, "You don't want to know!" That was all. That was it.

When the shock wore off, I realized I had to forgive. I had not let go. I was still pouting with pride, licking my wounds of hurt. Feeling self-pity I questioned, "How could they think that of me?" (All I've ever done is work with everyone's children.) "Why didn't they ask me where I was late at night? (Of course I was home with my husband and children.) "In twenty years, has anyone ever seen me hanging around any parking lot ever—day or night? (I don't have the time or the interest.)

But do you know what? None of that made any difference. The only thing that I was responsible for was my response, and it needed H-E-L-P! God had allowed the accusation for His purposes.

I prayed, "Thank you, Father, for rescuing me, for defending me, and for keeping me. Thank you for your lovingkindness and protection. Right now I choose to forgive those involved. God, I'm sorry for my bad attitude. Please replace it with your attitude of humility, joy, and acceptance. Even though I don't feel it, I am going to thank you for what happened. Somehow, someway, sometime, please use it for your honor and glory. And—dear Lord—I do pray that your church will be known by our love for one another."

Sure I'm vulnerable. Yes, I love to be loved, admired, and appreciated—especially by other Christians.

Satan knows that also. But I firmly believe that whatever our enemy means for evil, "God [means] it for good" (Genesis 50:20).

Loving other Christians is not a feeling. It is a choice. Forgiving other Christians is not an option. It is a necessity.

Christian Hurt—Crisis Steps to God-Confidence

1. Remember that our Lord knows all about rejection and humiliation. The Scriptures say that Jesus was "despised and rejected by men, a man of sorrows, and acquainted with grief" (Isaiah 53:3). Jesus was humiliated. He "endured the cross, despising the shame" (Hebrews 12:2).

2. Remember: God is who He says He is! And He knows what's best for us—but we must trust Him.

3. Thank the Lord for the trial that He has allowed for His purposes.

4. Choose to forgive those who have wounded and wronged you.

5. Ask the Lord to give you His love for other Christians!

———— ∽ ————

Over and over in this book we have observed as the Steps to God-confidence have been demonstrated in the lives of sensitive and vulnerable Christian women. We have shared their hurts, burdens, insecurities, and anxieties. We have witnessed the biblical and prayerful approach of these Christian heroines to Crisis Management. We have read about women who honestly reveal their weaknesses, but who have chosen to trust their powerful, faithful God.

There have been many stories, but only one message: God is worthy of our trust. The better we know Him, the more we will trust Him. And the more we trust Him, the more God-confidence we will have.

Reflections

1. Of the crises mentioned, which do you face most frequently? Least frequently?

_____

_____

_____

2. Look at the Crisis-Management Steps to God-Confidence for the crisis that you face most frequently. Which steps are easiest for you to apply? Which steps are the most difficult?

_____

_____

_____

_____

_____

_____

_____

_____

_____

3. How are you going to use these Crisis-Management Steps to God-Confidence in the future?

_____

_____

_____

_____

_____

4. What crisis is the most painful for you? Why?

_____

_____

_____

_____

5. How will the Crisis-Management Steps to God-Confidence help you during the turmoil of the next crisis?

_____

_____

_____

_____

6. Of all the stories that have been shared in this book, which three are the most personal and applicable to you?

_____

_____

_____

_____

7. How will you use the principles from this book as you encounter future crises?

"I Can't Trust God When I'm in a Crisis."

_____

_____

_____

_____

_____

Date of response_____

A Final Note

Every story included in this book is an outpouring of truth from the woman who has graciously shared it with us. In each instance, the response was: "If God can use my story to help even one woman, it will have been all worthwhile."

And if God can use my experiences and my foolish, inept words to help one insecure, seeking Christian woman, and lead her into a life of increasing God-confidence, this book will have meaning and purpose.

What about you? I believe that every Christian woman has at least one story to tell of hurt, sorrow, frustration, anxiety, or insecurity. I also know that Almighty God can do "exceedingly abundantly above all that we ask or think, according to the power that works in us" (Ephesians 3:20). I know this because of what His Word says, because of what He has done in the lives of the Christian women in this book, and because of what He has so graciously and mercifully done for me. And I am "confident of this very thing, that He who has begun a good work in you will complete it until the day of Jesus Christ" (Philippians 1:6).

God has allowed the earthquakes in your life. He has allowed your particular "treasure" to be shaken, broken, or torn from you for His purposes. Your "treasure" may have been body-image, health, accomplishment, management and control, things, men, or unscarred relationships with other believers. Martha Snell Nicholson describes the process of loss in her poem "Treasures":

> One by one He took them from me,
> All the things I valued most,
> Until I was empty-handed;
> Every glittering toy was lost.

And I walked earth's highways, grieving,
In my rags and poverty.
Till I heard His voice inviting,
"Lift your empty hands to Me!"

So I held my hands toward heaven,
And He filled them with a store
Of His own transcendent riches,
Till they could contain no more.

And at last I comprehended
With my stupid mind and dull,
That God could not pour His riches
Into hands already full![1]

—————— ∽ ——————

What is your story? How has God strengthened your God-confidence through loss? Write to me with your story:

> Pat Holt
> %Bethany House Publishers
> 11300 Hampshire Avenue S.
> Minneapolis, MN 55438

Acknowledgments

In my original concept of this book, I wanted to share some of what God has done in my life to transform my insecurities and lack of "self-esteem" into growing God-confidence.

But God's ways are much higher and better. You and I have witnessed that on every page. Rather than being my limited story, God chose to make this book an example of what happens when beautiful members of the body of Christ work harmoniously together.

Every baby step in the writing process has been a blessing. God provided sparkling Christian jewels who gave the book flesh and blood. Each one is a member of the body of Christ, and each contribution is unique and different. Isn't that just the way God works in His body?

My agent, Joyce Farrell, never fails to help and encourage. Thank you, Joyce!

Bethany House editor, David Hazard, graciously guided me over a period of months—patiently, persistently, and skillfully leading me step by step from the beginning to completion. Thank you, David!

My family is such a glorious gift from God! Each prayed and worked, then worked and prayed. Dave, my husband, always took time to listen, to help, to patiently and tirelessly guide me through the intricacies of my ever-present word processing dilemmas (not to mention the untold hours he spent making my messes reader friendly!). Even he could not fully comprehend how one human being could have such a plethora of persisting problems! Thank you, darling Dave!

My daughter, Candice, was also a part of the "Computer Help Line," for which I continue to be grateful. She never tired of listening to any portion of the manuscript, of making excellent suggestions, giving wise counsel, and important contributions. Thank you, dearest Candice.

My son, Gary, was the anchor man on the "Computer Help Line." His computer clues were accompanied with quips for clarity. Since I am a concordance cripple, his memory bank of references was invaluable. Thank you, dear Gary!

My "brother" Dale and his wife, Cindy, prayed and never failed to inquire with interest and concern. They provided the story of Mazie. Thank you, beloved ones.

My mom and dad prayed and checked on progress. They reminded me of the story of Tallah. Thank you for everything always!

My prayer partners are cherished above all expression of mere words. Sparkling prayer jewels, Liz George and Trudi Ponder, have heard about this proposed project for years and have faithfully prayed. The reality of this book shines as God's answer to their diligence. Thank you, cherished prayer warriors!

The entire West Valley Christian Academy staff, Board of Directors, and Moms-In-Touch prayer group are incomparable treasures in my life. They have prayed and prayed. They have always understood. They provide a little earthly glimpse of what heaven will be like. Some have graciously shared their heartbreaks and triumphs in this book. "I thank my God upon every remembrance of you" (Philippians 1:3).

The gracious Christian heroines, who shared their stories to help other women, remain in my heart with gratitude:

Chapter Two: Veronica, Jennifer, and Ruth. Chapter Three: Joni and Neva. Chapter Four: Jayni, Norma, Sharon, and Phyllis. Chapter Five: Pat Mac, Belinda, Candice, Mazie, Ruth Bell Graham, and Hannah Hurnard. Chapter Six: Beverly. Chapter Seven: Phyllis, and Debra, Jeanne, and Sara. Chapter Eight: Jayni, Norma, Marion, Melanie, Tallah, Dr. M. Lon Kasow, and Diana. Chapter

Nine: Melanie, Patsy Clairmont, Mildred, Sally, Carol, Missy, Emily and Fred, and Jan. Chapter Ten: Nell and Shari.

Thank you, dear reader, for selecting this book. I fervently pray that it will bring the shining reality of God-confidence into your life.

Notes

Chapter One

1. Jack Hayford, audio tape #03845, *Afterthoughts Amid Aftershocks*, Jude 20–21;24–25 (Van Nuys, California: Soundword Tape Ministry, 1994).
2. Craig Johnson, audio tape #786A, *Expectations* (Westlake, California: Bethel Christian Fellowship, 1994).
3. Psalm 46:1–3.
4. Edward Mote, "The Solid Rock."

Chapter Two

1. Gloria Steinem, *Revolution From Within* (Boston, Toronto, London: Little, Brown and Company, 1992), p. 6.
2. Dr. James Dobson, *What Wives Wish Their Husbands Knew About Women* (Wheaton: Tyndale House Publisher, Inc., 1975), pp. 19–21.
3. David A. Seamands, *Healing for Damaged Emotions* (Wheaton: Victor Books, 1981), p. 49.

Chapter Three

1. Nora Scott Kinzer, *Put Down and Ripped Off* (New York: Thomas Y. Crowell Company, 1977), pp. 25–26.
2. Kathy Henderson, "Learn to Love the Body," *McCall's* (New York: New York Times Company Women's Magazines, February 1993), pp. 128–129.
3. Ibid.
4. Ibid.
5. Deborah Blum, "Studies on Beauty Raise a Number of Ugly Findings," *San Francisco Sunday Examiner and Chronicle* (San Francisco: *San Francisco Sunday Examiner and Chronicle*, February 16, 1992), p. B–10.
6. Gloria Steinem, *Revolution From Within* (Boston, Toronto, London: Little, Brown and Company, 1992), p. 216.
7. Glamour Editorial Staff, "Do You Look Good Because You Want to?" *Glamour* magazine (New York: *Glamour*, November 1991), pp. 95–96.
8. Leslie George, "Your Love/Hate Relationship With Looking Good," *Glamour* Magazine (New York: *Glamour*, April 1992), pp. 222–227.
9. Kathrin Perutz, *Beyond the Looking Glass* (New York: William Morrow and Company, Inc., 1970), Preface.

10. Gloria Steinem, *Revolution From Within* (Boston, Toronto, London: Little, Brown and company, 1992), p. 231.
11. Ibid.
12. Joni Eareckson Tada, *Friendship UNLIMITED* (Wheaton: Harold Shaw Publishers, 1987), p. 10.
13. Neva Coyle, *Overcoming the Dieting Dilemma* (Minneapolis, Minnesota: Bethany House Publishers, 1991), 14–17, pp. 98–99. Used by permission.

Chapter Four

1. Judith Viorst, *Necessary Losses* (New York: Simon and Schuster, 1986), pp. 287–288.
2. Ray Beeson and Ranelda Mack Hunsicker, *The Hidden Price of Greatness* (Wheaton: Tyndale House Publishers, Inc., 1991), pp. 52–53.
3. Compiled by Tom Carter, *Spurgeon at His Best* (Grand Rapids: Baker Book House, 1988), p. 190.
4. Patsy Clairmont, *Normal Is Just a Setting on Your Dryer* (Colorado Springs: Focus on the Family Publishing, 1993), p. 9.
5. Compiled by Tom Carter, *Spurgeon at His Best* (Grand Rapids: Baker Book House, 1988), p. 208.
6. Ibid., p. 191.
7. Tim Hansel, *You Gotta Keep Dancin'* (Elgin: David C. Cook Publishing Co., 1985), p. 15.
8. Ibid., p. 54.
9. Ray Beeson and Ranelda Mack Hunsicker, *The Hidden Price of Greatness* (Wheaton: Tyndale House Publishers, Inc., 1991), p. 91.
10. Ibid., pp. 93–94.

Chapter Five

1. Watty Piper, *The Little Engine That Could* (New York: Scholastic Inc., 1961).
2. Charles Stanley, "When Facing Life's Mountains," *Tape No. AS127* (Atlanta: In Touch Ministries).
3. Tim Hansel, *You Gotta Keep Dancin'* (Elgin: David C. Cook Publishing Co., 1985), p. 15.
4. Ruth Bell Graham, *Prodigals and Those Who Love Them* (Colorado Springs: Focus on the Family Publishing, 1991), p. 132.
5. Hannah Hurnard, *Hinds' Feet on High Places* (Wheaton: Tyndale House Publishers, Inc., 1975), pp. 307–309.
6. Ray Beeson and Ranelda Mack Hunsicker, *The Hidden Price of Greatness* (Wheaton: Tyndale House Publishers, Inc., 1991), pp. 133–134.
7. Margaret Brown Klapthor and Helen Duprey Bullock, editors, *The First Ladies Cook Book* (New York: Parents Magazine Enterprises, 1982), pp. 133–134.
8. Ron Mehl, *Surprise Endings* (Sisters, Oregon: Multnomah, 1993), p. 75.

Chapter Six

1. Richard J. Foster, *Celebration of Discipline* (San Francisco: Harper & Row, Publishers, 1987), p. 70.
2. Richard J. Foster, *Freedom of Simplicity* (San Francisco: Harper and Row, Publishers, 1981), p. 87.
3. James Gilchrist Lawson, *Deeper Experiences of Famous Christians* (Anderson: The Warner Press, 1911), pp. 203–213.
4. Ibid.
5. Ibid.

Chapter Seven

1. Judith Viorst, *Alexander and the Terrible, Horrible, No Good, Very Bad Day* (New York: Scholastic, Inc.).
2. John W. Cowart, *People Whose F-A-I-T-H Got Them into T-R-O-U-B-L-E* (Downers Grove: InterVarsity Press, 1990), pp. 82–83.
3. W. L. Doughty, editor and arranger, *The Prayers of Susanna Wesley* (Grand Rapids: Zondervan Publishing House, 1987), p. vii.
4. Phillip Keller, *A Shepherd Looks at Psalm 23* (Grand Rapids: Zondervan Publishing House, 1976), pp. 20–21.
5. Richard J. Foster, *Celebration of Discipline* (San Francisco: Harper & Row, Publishers, 1987), p. 85.
6. Richard J. Foster, *Freedom of Simplicity* (San Francisco: Harper San Francisco, 1981), p. 77.
7. Ray Beeson and Ranelda Mack Hunsicker, *The Hidden Price of Greatness* (Wheaton: Tyndale House Publishers, Inc., 1991), pp. 161–167.

Chapter Eight

1. Peter Feldner, "Reflections of a Divorced Dad," *Focus on the Family* (Colorado Springs: Focus on the Family Publishing, June 1993).
2. Francis A. Schaeffer, *Genesis in Space and Time* (Downers Grove: InterVarsity Press, 1976), pp. 93–94.
3. Franz Delitzch, D.D., *A New Commentary on Genesis* (Minneapolis: Klock & Klock Christian Publishers, 1978), p. 166.
4. Harold G. Stigers, *A Commentary on Genesis* (Grand Rapids: Zondervan Publishing House, 1976), p. 80.
5. Horatius Bonar, *Thoughts on Genesis* (Grand Rapids: Kregel Publications, 1875), pp. 178–179.
6. Ray Beeson and Ranelda Mack Hunsicker, *The Hidden Price of Greatness* (Wheaton: Tyndale House Publishers, Inc., 1991), p. 16.
7. John W. Cowart, *People Whose F-A-I-T-H Got Them Into T-R-O-U-B-L-E* (Downers Grove: InterVarsity Press, 1990), p. 82.
8. Ibid., p. 85.
9. Ibid., p. 88.
10. Joseph Scriven, "What a Friend" *Inspiring Hymns* (Grand Rapids: Singspiration Sacred Music Publishers, 1951), p. 384.
11. Elizabeth Prentiss, *Stepping Heavenward* (Amityville: Calvary Press, 1993), pp. 100–101.
12. Ibid., p. 218.

13. Ibid.
14. Ibid., Preface.

Chapter Nine

1. Patsy Clairmont, *Normal Is Just a Setting on Your Dryer* (Colorado Springs: Focus on the Family Publishing, 1993), pp. 103–104.
2. Ibid., p. 105.
3. Ray Beeson and Ranelda Mack Hunsicker, *The Hidden Price of Greatness* (Wheaton: Tyndale House Publishers, Inc., 1991), p. 29.
4. Ibid., p. 29.
5. Ibid.
6. Charles Stanley, *Forgiveness* (Nashville: Thomas Nelson Publishers, 1987), p. 133.

Chapter Ten

1. James Gilchrist Lawson, *Deeper Experiences of Famous Christians* (Anderson: Warner Press, 1911), p. 75.
2. Ibid., p. 78.
3. Ibid., p. 82.
4. *In Touch* Editor, "Meeting God at Every Turn," *In Touch* Magazine (Atlanta: In Touch Ministries, September 1993), pp. 8–9.

A Final Note

1. Martha Snell Nicholson, *Treasures* (Pensacola, Florida: A Beka Book, 1992), p. 9.